**New Directions for
Child and Adolescent
Development**

Lene Arnett Jensen
Reed W. Larson
EDITORS-IN-CHIEF

William Damon
FOUNDING EDITOR

D1525570

The Development of Autobiographical Reasoning in Adolescence and Beyond

Tilmann Habermas

EDITOR

Number 131 • Spring 2011
Jossey-Bass
San Francisco

THE DEVELOPMENT OF AUTOBIOGRAPHICAL REASONING IN ADOLESCENCE
AND BEYOND
Tilmann Habermas (ed.)
New Directions for Child and Adolescent Development, no. 131
Lene Arnett Jensen, Reed W. Larson, Editors-in-Chief

Microfilm copies of issues and articles are available in 16mm and 35mm, as well as microfiche in 105mm, through University Microfilms, Inc., 300 North Zeeb Road, Ann Arbor, Michigan 48106-1346.

ISSN 1520-3247   electronic ISSN 1534-8687

NEW DIRECTIONS FOR CHILD AND ADOLESCENT DEVELOPMENT is part of The Jossey-Bass Education Series and is published quarterly by Wiley Subscription Services, Inc., a Wiley company, at Jossey-Bass, 989 Market Street, San Francisco, California 94103-1741. Periodicals postage paid at San Francisco, California, and at additional mailing offices. Postmaster: Send address changes to New Directions for Child and Adolescent Development, Jossey-Bass, 989 Market Street, San Francisco, CA 94103-1741.

New Directions for Child and Adolescent Development is indexed in Cambridge Scientific Abstracts (CSA/CIG), CHID: Combined Health Information Database (NIH), Contents Pages in Education (T&F), Current Abstracts (EBSCO), Educational Research Abstracts Online (T&F), EMBASE/Excerpta Medica (Elsevier), ERIC Database (Education Resources Information Center), Index Medicus/MEDLINE/PubMed (NLM), Linguistics & Language Behavior Abstracts (CSA/CIG), Psychological Abstracts/PsycINFO (APA), Social Services Abstracts (CSA/CIG), SocINDEX (EBSCO), and Sociological Abstracts (CSA/CIG).

SUBSCRIPTION rates: For the U.S., $89 for individuals and $315 for institutions. Please see ordering information page at end of journal.

EDITORIAL CORRESPONDENCE should be e-mailed to the editors-in-chief: Lene Arnett Jensen (ljensen@clarku.edu) and Reed W. Larson (larsonr@illinois.edu).

Jossey-Bass Web address: www.josseybass.com

CONTENTS

Habermas, T. (2010). Autobiographical reasoning: Arguing and narrating from a biographical perspective. In T. Habermas (Ed.) The development of autobiographical reasoning in adolescence and beyond. *New Directions for Child and Adolescent Development, 131*, 1–17.

1

Autobiographical Reasoning: Arguing and Narrating from a Biographical Perspective

Tilmann Habermas

Abstract

Autobiographical reasoning is the activity of creating relations between different parts of one's past, present, and future life and one's personality and development. It embeds personal memories in a culturally, temporally, causally, and thematically coherent life story. Prototypical autobiographical arguments are presented. Culture and socializing interactions shape the development of autobiographical reasoning especially in late childhood and adolescence. Situated at the intersection of cognitive and narrative development and autobiographical memory, autobiographical reasoning contributes to the development of personality and identity, is instrumental in efforts to cope with life events, and helps to create a shared history. © Wiley Periodicals, Inc.

Thanks to Verena Diel for critical comments on this chapter and to Anna Kenney and Andrea Silberstein for their editorial help with the volume, and to Susan Bluck with whom I first developed the concept of autobiographical reasoning.

Hermann Ebbinghaus lay the foundations for the psychology of memory in 1880 by substituting everyday remembering with an experimental paradigm that focused on the controlled learning of elements with identical value, the correct remembering of which could therefore be counted and related to the passing of time. These elements were to have no links, neither to words nor to things; they were designed to have no prior meaning (Ebbinghaus, 1983). This paradigm defined memory psychology for an entire century, with a few important exceptions such as work by Bartlett (1932). Maybe the most outspoken antipode to Ebbinghaus was his colleague at the University of Berlin, Wilhelm Dilthey (1895), who proclaimed life stories as the model for the *Geisteswissenschaften*, the humanities, which approach their subject through historical understanding. Life stories center on emergent meaning, not numbers. Linking the events within a life to each other and the individual's overall development, and embedding this life in a social and historical context, endows the life with meaning. Wilhelm Dilthey was not interested in memory, but in obtaining the most exhaustive information possible about phenomena that need to be understood in the light of their history.

Psychology began to leave Ebbinghaus's "memorizing trap" (Danziger, 2008) only a century later, moving one step in the direction of Dilthey by developing an interest in everyday remembering instead of memorizing laboratory material (Neisser, 1982). This new object of psychological research was termed *autobiographical memory* (Rubin, 1986). Psychologists, interested in the representation of temporally structured knowledge, took a further step in the direction of Dilthey's interest in the life story by introducing narrative as the central form for organizing and communicating events (Nelson & Gruendel, 1981).

Everyday remembering of single events involves varying degrees of linking, contextualizing, and interpreting. One kind of linking consists of creating the temporal, spatial, and social context of the remembered episode. In narratives, this is the purpose of the initial orientation section. Another kind of linking is of a more linear nature and consists of linking actions and events by putting them in a temporal-causal order that makes sense to the rememberer and the listener alike. In narratives, this is the purpose of explanations and narrative clauses, the sequence of which imitates the sequence of events. Except for some involuntary memories (cf. Berntsen, 2009), everyday remembering is an active, reconstructive activity that involves at least some degree of argumentative linking, or narrative reasoning (Rubin & Greenberg, 2003).

In this volume, we take the next step in the direction of Dilthey's life-historical approach to memory and individuality, by focusing on narratives of memories, not of any everyday events, but on past, present, and future events that are of biographical relevance. Biographical relevance marks aspects of one's past that have meaning for one's life, and therefore would justifiably enter one's written autobiography. These meaningful events are contextualized by life, linked not only by chronological order, but also by arguments that state thematic or causal-motivational implications, similarities, or consequences. Habermas and Bluck (2000) coined the term *autobiographical reasoning* for this activity of explicating the biographical relevance of memories. Autobiographical reasoning creates links between remembered events and other distant parts of one's life and to the self and its development. It refers to the remembering subject's life as the relevant frame of reference, thereby implying the life story. Autobiographical reasoning requires extra mental effort that goes beyond the effort of mere remembering. We termed this activity as *reasoning* to underscore three aspects: the constructive and interpretative nature of the activity, the both cognitive and communicative nature of it, and its normative aspect implied by its appeal to reason and logic. The term reasoning also alludes to the cognitive-developmental tradition (Piaget, 1924), which we wed to the narrative tradition. Related constructs are those of the *life review* (Butler, 1963), *identity-related reminiscing* (Webster, 1993), and *reflecting on life* (Pasupathi, Weeks, & Rice, 2006; Staudinger, 2001) because they tend to require reference to the whole life.

Autobiographical reasoning is a late acquisition in socio-cognitive development, as it begins to develop only in preadolescence and continues to mature throughout adolescence. This development draws remembering closer to the self, maximizing identity implications of remembered episodes by linking them to individual development. Only the ability for autobiographical reasoning allows individuals to understand what it means when they are asked for self-defining memories.

This volume demonstrates how a focus on this late maturing competence opens new perspectives in the psychology of adolescence. This introductory chapter contextualizes the main arguments of the following chapters. First, I will outline the conceptual life story framework of which autobiographical reasoning is a part and then present some prototypical arguments used in autobiographical reasoning. Then I will discuss what is known to date about the development of the ability for autobiographical reasoning in adolescence and age differences in its spontaneous use across adulthood. As autobiographical reasoning is conceived as a basically socio-cognitive process, I will then discuss which cultural models influence autobiographical reasoning, and which socializing narrative and discursive practices may shape autobiographical reasoning especially in adolescence. Finally, I will review mostly indirect evidence on how autobiographical reasoning is adaptive in different contexts. This introduction and the following chapters take a strong theoretical stance, mapping new areas for research in adolescence and beyond. The introduction closes with a brief presentation of each chapter.

NEW DIRECTIONS FOR CHILD AND ADOLESCENT DEVELOPMENT • DOI: 10.1002/cd

Autobiographical Reasoning Builds and Uses the Life Story

We conceived of autobiographical reasoning as one of two possible manifestations of the autobiographical life story, the other being entire life narratives. An essential aspect of the life story is its global coherence. Its parts
are related to each other and to the whole; events are related to other
events and to the development of the individual. We highlighted four
kinds of global coherence of special relevance to the life story. First, life
stories are constructed following more or less a *cultural concept of biography*, which we defined as a skeletal structure of temporally ordered biographically salient life events with age norms attached to them (Habermas
& Bluck, 2000). This sequence of life events was termed *life script* by
Berntsen and Rubin (2004). It represents a normative cultural life course
(Neugarten, Moore, & Lowe, 1965). Other aspects of the cultural concept
of biography concern not how life is to be lived, but how life is to be narrated, such as how to begin and end a life narrative (Habermas, Ehlert-
Lerche, & de Silveira, 2009). Second, *global temporal coherence* allows the
listener to locate events in the narrator's life. The most basic temporal
order of events in narratives is chronological. Artful narrators may deviate
from this pattern, but to maintain global temporal coherence they need to
mark deviations from chronological time (Habermas et al., 2009). Third,
global causal-motivational coherence provides a sense of direction and purpose to a life. Life narratives vary in the degree to which events are pur-
ported to be caused externally or motivated by one's desires, aims, and
values (Schafer, 1983). Causal-motivational coherence bridges change,
connecting what had been earlier and what became of it, most notably the
narrator's person and personality. Fourth, *global thematic coherence* is
established by extracting continuities across change. Global coherence is
what differentiates the life story from mere lists of unrelated memories
from one's life.

Whereas entire life narratives are usually only produced in research
interviews, in everyday life the life story is usually manifested in the more
partial form of autobiographical reasoning. We suggested that repeated
autobiographical reasoning leads to the construction of a rudimentary
knowledge structure in memory that relates to life as a whole, termed *life
story schema*, which in turn is activated and used in autobiographical
reasoning. Thus, autobiographical reasoning may involve arguments constructed on the spot, which are then saved as an enduring knowledge
structure. It may also use arguments already stored in memory, such as the
product of earlier autobiographical reasoning. In the process of autobiographical reasoning, past events may be remembered and are then interpreted by putting them in a biographical context (Bluck & Habermas,
2000). Despite obvious motivational differences, autobiographical reasoning is structurally identical with biographical reasoning about another

individual's life because it takes an external, third-person perspective of a life. This structural homology shows both in studies of the memory of and reasoning about literary representations of life in novels and short stories (Copeland, Radvansky & Goodwin, 2009; Feldman, Bruner, Kalmar, & Renderer, 1993; Genereux & McKeough, 2007; Mar & Oatley, 2008), as well as in clinical practice. Psychoanalysts construct life stories of their patients to identify recurrent themes and conflicts, and to explain these developmentally as responses to specific experiences and to developing motives and conflicts. In principle, this kind of reconstruction is structurally homologous to how patients themselves may narrate and explain their lives (Linde, 1993; Schafer, 1983).

Prototypical Autobiographical Arguments

Autobiographical reasoning often involves some of the following prototypical arguments (Habermas & Paha, 2001; cf. Pasupathi, & Weeks, Chapter Three; Fivush, Bohanek, & Zaman, Chapter Four, for additional autobiographical arguments). I shall first describe arguments that bridge change, then arguments that establish continuity. They are arguments insofar as they provide reasons for claims or causes for states of affairs.

   Biographical Change. The following list of autobiographical arguments ranges from very basic to more complex references to biography. A normative idea of the life course may be invoked by referring to the *developmental status* of an individual to explain his or her reaction, ability, or sensibility (McCabe, Capron, & Peterson, 1991), such as in "My parents' divorce didn't affect me much. I wasn't really aware of what was happening. I was still too little." In a more individual vein, specific experiences may be said to have had a *formative influence* on the individual, for example, by stating the influence of a role model. More individual influences of specific events on the development of personality can be designated as *events causing personality change*, such as in "After age ten, I became a shy person because the separation of my parents made me distrust others." An experience may also have a more specific influence in creating a sensibility or motivation to react in a specific way in specific kinds of situations (Feldman et al., 1993). This very typical biographical argument is used to explain strange behaviors by reference to the *biographical background* of the individual, such as in "When a car suddenly raced towards us, he panicked. He had been run over by a car when he was small." Events may also be causally related to long-term *biographical consequences*, such as changes in life circumstances, relationships, or later events. Mackavey, Malley, and Stewart (1991) identified events in the written autobiographies of forty-nine psychologists that were explicitly named as biographically consequential. They most frequently came from early adulthood. A specific linguistic form to point out biographical consequences is a *past–present* *comparison* that states that something is different *ever since* a specified event happened.

An especially important set of biographical arguments regards change in the individual's knowledge and understanding, evaluations, and intentions. A simple way for an event to change an individual's outlook is to provide new information. An increase in knowledge is often expressed negatively by stating that at a specific point in life one had not yet known something, or by verbs like *finding out*. Experiences in which *an aspect of personality is revealed* belong to this category if the assumption is that the aspect has always been there, for instance the metaphor of *coming out* implies a process of revelation of sexual orientation (cf. Pasupathi & Weeks, Chapter Three). A more active change in outlook is brought about when the individual *learns a lesson*. An experience is related to a lasting understanding of a mechanism and how to better deal with a specific situation, like when a twelve-year-old boy states, "That's why I told myself, next time I fall in love, school work should not suffer from it." The individual actively processes an experience, but the inferences drawn remain limited to circumscribed situations. The most profound process of understanding is involved in *general insights*. The individual generalizes a single experience to a very general rule of how the world works, as in this insight of a fifteen-year-old girl: "I was really emotionally hooked up with him for a long time. Probably that's what always happens when it's the first kiss" (Habermas & Paha, 2001; cf. McLean & Thorne, 2003). These biographical arguments that relate an experience to a change in the subjective outlook usually imply an increase in understanding and insight.

Biographical Continuity. Thematic coherence is most often constructed hierarchically, by creating a higher-level category that integrates more specific categories or instances. By assimilating diverse, temporally distributed local elements of a life to an overarching concept, continuity is created. A major device in autobiographical narratives is *exemplification*. A general statement covering an extended period, for example, about one's personality, may be substantiated by providing an episode in which this trait is manifested. A formally similar argument is used to *explain specific actions by the actor's personality*. Whereas exemplifications start from a general, abstract claim that is then exemplified, explanations of actions by personality are adduced within the context of a specific episode—they proceed from the particular (explanandum) to the general (explanans). Pasupathi, Mansour, and Brubaker (2007) pointed to an interesting variation of the argument, namely negating that an action can be explained by a trait, by stating that an action is atypical for the self, thereby safeguarding self-continuity against events that disrupt continuity. Another way to highlight stability is to state that something is *still the same today*. Finally, *parallels may be constructed between a specific episode and other episodes*. Thus, narrators frequently state that a given kind of experience happened to them more than once, or that it was a typical experience. In this case, it

NEW DIRECTIONS FOR CHILD AND ADOLESCENT DEVELOPMENT • DOI: 10.1002/cd

is not an abstract trait, but a class of episodes or pattern of experiences that is stable.

Development of Autobiographical Reasoning

We have reviewed probable developmental prerequisites of autobiographical reasoning (Habermas & Bluck, 2000). Briefly stated, autobiographical reasoning joins the categorical concept of person with the temporal structure of event representations (cf. Nelson & Gruendel, 1981), socio-cognitive with narrative development. Older grade school children and preadolescents know how to narrate single episodes (Peterson & McCabe, 1994), and they have developed a complex person concept organized in terms of abstract dispositions that explain more specific habits and attitudes (Selman, 1980). Only during adolescence, however, do they learn to conceive of individuals in biographical terms, contextualizing personality in individual development that bridges personal discontinuities in increasingly sophisticated ways (Chandler, Lalonde, Sokol, & Hallett, 2003; Selman, 1980). Therefore, it is only in adolescence that coherent life narratives can be constructed. Wedding the neo-Piagetian cognitive-developmental theory of Case (1985) with narrative developmental theory, Anne McKeough and Genereux (2003) showed a significant increase of interpretative biographical abilities between ages ten and eighteen (cf. McKeough & Malcolm, Chapter Five). In an exploratory (Habermas & Paha, 2001) and two larger studies of entire life narratives—oral narratives spanning ages eight to twenty (Habermas & de Silveira, 2008) and written narratives spanning ages nine to fifteen (Bohn & Berntsen, 2008)—globally coherent life stories were absent in older children and gradually emerged across early and mid-adolescence. The studies used a variety of measures of global coherence, from relative frequencies of autobiographical reasoning and global coherence ratings to codes of the autobiographical well-formedness of beginnings and endings and judgments of the overall narrative structure.

The spontaneous use of autobiographical reasoning appears to increase beyond adolescence. In a life-span study of narratives of wisdom-related events, the spontaneous creation of causal links to other life events increased across adulthood, and drawing a lesson from this experience increased between adolescence and middle adulthood (Bluck & Glück, 2004). Another element of autobiographical reasoning, creating causal links between biographical events and the self and personal development, increased in crisis narratives across adulthood (Pasupathi & Mansour, 2006). In a study by McLean (2008), however, younger and older adults did not differ in the frequency of self-event connections in narratives of self-defining memories.

Apart from identifying autobiographical reasoning as elements of life narratives, Habermas, Fröhlich, and Diel (2009) devised a separate semi-structured Autobiographical Reasoning Interview to test for the spontaneous tendency of and the ability to use autobiographical reasoning. The interview elicits a narrative of an important life event, and then asks for specific factual and counterfactual causal-motivational links, as well as for thematic links between the event and other events or the narrator's self. This research team found a dramatic increase in autobiographical links provided between late childhood and mid-adolescence. The increase showed both in spontaneous autobiographical reasoning as well as in the generally higher maximal competence as demonstrated in responses to probing.

Cultural Models

Whereas narrative is a universal format to share experiences and event knowledge, the life story may not be universal. The prototypical Western developmental life story is derived from literary autobiographies and dates back only to the eighteenth century to works such as Rousseau's *Confessions*. In a cross-cultural comparison, some cultures seem to demand more telling of life stories and autobiographical reasoning than others (Tonkin, 1992). Western cultures appear to stress remembering of personal experiences and elaborations of the personal point of view at least for single experiences (e.g., Wang, 2004). Given this historical and cultural variation, it is plausible to assume that what is considered a good life story also varies with culture. In Europe, knowledge about the normative skeletal version of a life in terms of biographically salient life events and their age norms is acquired during early to mid-adolescence, not as a consequence of experiencing these events, but as a unitary concept stretching across life (Bohn & Berntsen, 2008; Habermas, 2007). Knowledge of the life script also correlates with the global coherence of life narratives (cf. Bohn, Chapter Two) and with both causal and thematic autobiographical reasoning (Habermas et al., 2009).

There may be different pathways for acquiring this cultural knowledge and ability. One could be the use of cultural media such as watching talk shows on TV or reading biographies and novels. There are strong arguments that reading fiction helps to develop an understanding of human motives and empathy (Mar & Oatley, 2008). Mar, Peskin, and Fong (Chapter Six) point out that reading about the lives of others may elicit a self-centered reading that draws parallels between protagonists' lives or narrators' interpretations and the understanding of one's own life. Novels may serve especially as a model for constructing an extended life story in its temporal-causal ordering. Mar and colleagues also make a strong point by noting that poetry may foster readers' ability and propensity to find metaphors, helping to create thematic coherence in a life. This resonates with some of the excerpts of family stories reported by McKeough and Malcolm in Chapter Five in which the older adolescents use metaphors to integrate characteristic aspects. In our Autobiographical Reasoning Interview, the central question for thematic links asks for a red thread or overarching theme of one's life, i.e., for metaphors. Accordingly, the frequency of a youth's participation in biographical practices such as writing diaries or letters, or reading biographies correlates with the temporal global coherence and the well-formedness of endings of life narratives (Habermas & de Silveira, 2008; Habermas et al., 2009) as well as with temporal autobiographical reasoning (Habermas et al., 2009).

Socializing Narrative Practices

A more direct way to acquire the cultural concept of biography may be by participating in socializing interactions with more cognitively mature and competent members of a culture. Basic narrative ability is acquired in memory talk with adults who help young children structure their memories by heavy scaffolding (Fivush, Haden, & Reese, 2006). Although adolescents are much more autonomous than preschool children and do participate in the wider culture on their own, talk about the past is still very much shared with parents and the family. Fivush and colleagues (Chapter Four) show that spontaneous talk about the shared past is quite frequent in families. Reminiscing in families need not involve autobiographical reasoning and will often consist of mere mutual confirmation of a shared past. However, what Fivush and colleagues call *intergenerational narratives*—parents' narratives about their own lives—often evoke autobiographical reasoning on the part of adolescents who draw parallels between their own and their parent's life, or point to how parents' advice is rooted in their life experience. The kind of naturalistic research on everyday talk presented by Fivush and colleagues is a necessary, but starkly underrepresented approach to psychological phenomena.

Although parent–child dialogues studied in the laboratory cannot provide information about the spontaneous use of autobiographical reasoning, they do tell us something about how parents and adolescents may talk to each other. Pasupathi and Weeks (Chapter Three) provide illuminative excerpts from mother–daughter dialogues in which the mother crafts a continuous personality of the daughter that stretches from the past into the future. They also show how a mother challenges her adolescent daughter's self-understanding, arguing for the stability of her personality, based also on her advantage of knowing the daughter's distant past better than the daughter herself does. Pasupathi and Weeks hypothesize that parents may enable their children to discover continuities, whereas peers as listeners might be better suited to emphasize change and development.

How the stories that are repeatedly told in families, termed *family stories*, are digested by adolescents according to their cognitive development is demonstrated in the contribution by Anne McKeough and Jennifer

Malcolm (Chapter Five). With a clinical interview following up on the re-narration of a family story, the authors show how older children stick to a literal interpretation of the story, whereas preadolescents draw a moral from the story, and mid-adolescents excerpt some overarching insight that applies not only to the adolescent, but to lives in general. Thus as adolescents mature cognitively, they increasingly interpret biographical stories they hear from their parents and integrate them into their view of their own (and their parents') lives by means of the developing ability for autobiographical reasoning. McKeough and Malcolm show how general cognitive abilities are applied to fictional narratives and, more specifically, to family narratives pertaining to their own lives. They thus succeed in relating general social-cognitive development to narrative development and autobiographical reasoning.

Although longitudinal studies of the effects of shared parental autobiographical reasoning on adolescents' ability for autobiographical reasoning are lacking, there is at least some evidence that mothers adapt to the growth of the child's and adolescent's ability for autobiographical reasoning by supporting abilities that their child is only about to learn. Preadolescents first learn to temporally structure a life story with the help of the life script, and only later learn to construct causal-motivational and thematic coherence in life narratives by relating life events to each other and the self (Habermas & de Silveira, 2008). Accordingly, in an exploratory study of life stories co-narrated by sixteen mothers and their children, in late childhood and preadolescence mothers supported temporal autobiographical reasoning, whereas in early and mid-adolescence they supported causal-motivational reasoning that focused on personality and its development (Habermas, Negele, & Brenneisen-Mayer, in press).

Functions and Adaptivity of Autobiographical Reasoning

The ability to create coherence and continuity in one's life story is normatively expected from adult members of Western cultures and contributes to a mature and healthy psycho-social identity (Erikson, 1968). This seems to suggest that autobiographical reasoning is beneficial by helping to integrate diverse aspects of one's past and personality into a coherent and continuous self. Fivush, Bohanek, and Zaman (Chapter Four) provide evidence that adolescents whose mothers are involved in co-narrating distant memories with them have less psychological symptoms. Pennebaker and colleagues found that repeatedly writing about a traumatic event with increasing causal connections and words indicating insight is related to better physical health (Pennebaker, Mayne, & Francis, 1997; cf. Frattaroli, 2006). In a study more directly related to the life story, a composite measure of narrative coherence for significant life memories correlated with measures of well-being (Baerger & McAdams, 1999). One of the four criteria of coherence had been whether the event was explicitly related to other parts of the narrator's life. In a four-year longitudinal study, an increase in emotional health correlated with causal reasoning in narratives of personality change at the end of these four years (Lodi-Smith et al., 2009).

The Adult Attachment Interview (AAI; Main, Kaplan, & Cassidy, 1985) also seems to suggest that autobiographical reasoning reflects psychological health. It is a semi-structured biographical interview that measures attachment security as communicative coherence in the sense that abstract claims and concrete examples for one's past relationships are adequately and convincingly expressed. Although the AAI aims at eliciting autobiographical reasoning, it is not the frequency of autobiographical reasoning but its quality that is relevant for the categorization of attachment security. Accordingly, in a reanalysis of AAI transcripts of twenty-seven young women (cf. Gloger-Tippelt, Gomille, König, & Vetter, 2002), we found no differences between securely and insecurely attached women in terms of relative frequencies of the use of autobiographical arguments and exemplifications (Höpfner, 2007). Similarly, life narratives of clinically depressed in-patients did not contain less autobiographical arguments than those of matched controls (Habermas, Ott, Schubert, Schneider, & Pate, 2008). Some authors even argue that, at least with regard to traumatic experiences, it is detrimental to psychological health to integrate these experiences into one's life story (Berntsen & Rubin, 2007). McLean and Mansfield (Chapter Seven) review evidence from their own and others' research that the adaptivity of autobiographical reasoning may vary with context, content, and age. A promising suggestion of theirs is that one precondition for autobiographical reasoning to be helpful is that one is sufficiently mature enough to adequately reason autobiographically and not just to ruminate about past events.

From a clinical perspective, detrimental effects could be expected from too intellectual uses of autobiographical reasoning that only serve to suppress emotions. In addition, repetitive ruminating about the same negative aspects of the past is a symptom of depression. Treynor, Gonzalez, and Nolen-Hoeksema (2003) found that brooding over negative consequences of depression predicted an increase in depression, whereas reflecting upon possible reasons for one's depression predicted a decrease. Other aspects of autobiographical reasoning which may impact how beneficial it is are whether it is used for solving a specific problem or not (see McLean and Mansfield, Chapter Seven) and whether it is used in solitary thinking or in communication with others.

In a way, autobiographical reasoning may be beneficial to the degree that it is normative. I do not intend this to mean that the life story needs to follow conventional conceptions, although in a Danish sample a conventional life correlated negatively with depressiveness, but not so in a U.S. sample (Rubin, Berntsen, & Hutson, 2009) nor in a German sample

(Habermas, Negele, Arslan, & Tavenaux, 2008). Rather, autobiographical reasoning might be beneficial if it fulfills a criterion that transcends the formal definition adopted here, that is, if it follows communicative norms to adhere to common sense so that listeners may find it plausible and reasonable.

The concept of autobiographical reasoning is intended to bridge the radical gap between Ebbinghaus and Dilthey. Our conception of memory starts with everyday remembering that is both linguistic and meaningful, embedded in dialogue and relationships, and influenced by wishes and their biographical roots. We thus suggest to keep our theoretical conception of memory as complex as necessary to do justice to the phenomena of interest. Methodologically, case studies that allow apprehending the complexities of specific contexts and individual lives are a rich and necessary part of psychological research (e.g., Larsen & Hansen, 2005). Memory is narrative if it is successful. However, and this is what we retain from the Ebbinghaus tradition, we have an interest in empirically based generalizations of psychological insight, which requires systematic empirical comparison. For these purposes, it is important that the concept of autobiographical reasoning allows some degree of quantification.

Overview of the Volume

This volume has been composed to offer an overview of relevant developmental research on autobiographical reasoning to date and to integrate contributions from memory, cognitive developmental, narrative, discourse, identity, literary, and coping perspectives, and to present conceptual advances. In the course of this volume, the perspective on autobiographical reasoning gradually expands, starting with a focus on the individual, opening up to interactions and the family, to the wider culture via literature, and ending with a shift of focus on the consequences of autobiographical reasoning.

In Chapter Two, Annette Bohn argues for the central role of the cultural life script in creating coherence in life stories. Global coherence of written life narratives correlates with the acquisition of the life script. The latter, however, does not correlate with coherence in single-event narratives, underlining the difference between stories and life stories. Bohn exemplifies the interplay between the personal and the prescriptive cultural form by contrasting the presumed life narrative of a nine-year-old boy with his life narrative three years later, which corresponds much better to what we expect a life story to read like.

In Chapter Three, Monisha Pasupathi and Trisha Weeks define the core of autobiographical reasoning as the act of establishing links between events in time and the self-concept. They present a system of this kind of autobiographical argument that they term *self-event relations*. These can be identified in narratives of single autobiographical memories. The authors

NEW DIRECTIONS FOR CHILD AND ADOLESCENT DEVELOPMENT • DOI: 10.1002/cd

argue that these arguments serve the identity function of establishing personal continuity across change. Building on Pasupathi's earlier work on listener effects on autobiographical memory and expanding Fivush's work on mother–child memory talk in preschool children to adolescence, the authors then develop ideas on how socializing interactions might support adolescents' emerging ability for autobiographical reasoning. Excerpts from mother–daughter discussions of the adolescent's personal development illustrate these ideas.

In Chapter Four, Robyn Fivush, Jennifer Bohanek, and Widaad Zaman focus on how narrating in families supports adolescents developing life story and self-concept, and how it supports their well-being. Exceptionally daring for psychologists, they analyze naturally occurring dinner table conversations in families with adolescents. Only this kind of data can show how relevant narratives are in real life. Indeed, narratives make up not the majority of ongoing family talk, but a substantial part of it. Most interestingly, intergenerational stories about the parents' lives prior to their children's recollection were surprisingly frequent. Interviewed individually about intergenerational narratives, adolescents were easily able to provide such stories from both their parents' lives and, by way of autobiographical reasoning, to intertwine them with their own life story. In addition, interesting gender differences emerged.

In Chapter Five, Anne McKeough and Jennifer Malcolm present their work on how social-cognitive development (in terms of Case's neo-Piagetian theory) is applied to the understanding of and drawing inferences from fictional stories across adolescence, thereby bridging cognitive and narrative development. They then go on to show that parallel to general cognitive development and to the development of understanding fictional stories, adolescents develop an understanding of family stories that are told repeatedly by parents. In re-narrations of these stories and subsequent clinical interviews, adolescents show a progressing ability for autobiographical reasoning by interpreting the stories and excerpting a moral from them also with the use of metaphor. The authors bridge both general cognitive development and narrative understanding, as well as the understanding of fictional and real-life stories.

In Chapter Six, Raymond Mar, Joan Peskin, and Katrina Fong write about a much-neglected topic in psychology, the meaning and possible effects of fictional literature on the minds and lives of adolescents. They eloquently argue for the role that reading fiction has in developing an understanding of how lives are constructed, of how motivation and personality develop biographically, and of how individuals may remain the same despite change. Second, they also provide strong arguments for why reading poetry may enhance adolescents' abilities to extract themes from a life and to create thematic coherence using metaphor. Despite the lack of direct evidence, the authors succeed in constructing indirect evidence from this much under-researched field of psychology that can actually be read as a call for future studies that directly test the possible influence of reading literature.

In Chapter Seven, Kate McLean and Cade Mansfield move from the different manifestations and the development of autobiographical reasoning to the possible effects of autobiographical reasoning. I believe that it is not only a dearly held conviction of psychoanalysts, but also a fundamental belief of many educated people, which is deeply rooted in European and American intellectual and cultural tradition, that trying to understand yourself and your life is both morally required and good for yourself and others. McLean and Mansfield partially undermine this assumption by discussing evidence that at least limits its validity. They argue that in some circumstances, in some social contexts, and at specific ages, autobiographical reasoning might be detrimental rather than beneficial to the individual. The authors show that once the core concept and the main developmental line of autobiographical reasoning have been established, studying multiple uses in different contexts will be the next step to take.

References

Baerger, D. R., & McAdams, D. P. (1999). Life story coherence and its relation to psychological well-being. *Narrative Inquiry, 9,* 69–96.

Bartlett, F. W. (1932). *Remembering: A study in experimental and social psychology.* London: Cambridge University Press.

Berntsen, D. (2009). *Involuntary autobiographical memories.* Oxford: Oxford University Press.

Berntsen, D., & Rubin, D. C. (2004). Cultural life scripts structure recall from autobiographical memory. *Memory & Cognition, 32,* 427–442.

Berntsen, D., & Rubin, D. C. (2007). When a trauma becomes a key to identity: Enhanced integration of trauma memories predicts posttraumatic stress disorder symptoms. *Applied Cognitive Psychology, 21,* 417–431.

Bluck, S., & Glück, J. (2004). Making things better and learning a lesson: Experiencing wisdom across the lifespan. *Journal of Personality, 72,* 543–572.

Bluck, S., & Habermas, T. (2000). The life story schema. *Motivation and Emotion, 24,* 121–147.

Bohn, A. (2010). Normative ideas of life and autobiographical reasoning in life narratives. In T. Habermas (Ed.), The development of autobiographical reasoning in adolescence and beyond. *New Directions for Child and Adolescent Development, 131,* 19–30.

Bohn, A., & Berntsen, D. (2008). Life story development in childhood: The development of life story abilities and the acquisition of cultural life scripts from late middle childhood to adolescence. *Developmental Psychology, 44,* 1135–1142.

Butler, R. (1963). The life review: An interpretation of reminiscence in the aged. *Psychiatry, 26,* 65–76.

Case, R. (1985). *Intellectual development: Birth to adulthood.* Toronto: Academic Press.

Chandler, M. J., Lalonde, C. E., Sokol, B. W., & Hallett, D. (2003). Personal persistence, identity development, and suicide: A study of native and non-native North American adolescents. *Monographs of the Society for Research in Child Development, 68,* 1–138.

Copeland, D. E., Radvansky, G. A., & Goodwin, K. A. (2009). A novel study: Forgetting curves and the reminiscence bump. *Memory, 17*, 323–336.

Danziger, K. (2008). *Marking the mind: The history of memory.* Cambridge, England: Cambridge University Press.

Dilthey, W. (1895). Über eine beschreibende und zergliedernde Psychologie [On a descriptive and an analytical psychology]. In W. Dilthey (Ed.), *Gesammelte Schriften* [Collected Writings] (Vol. 5, pp. 139–240). Stuttgart, Göttingen: Teubner, Vandenhoeck & Rupprecht.

Ebbinghaus, H. (1983). Urmanuskript "Über das Gedächtnis" [Original manuscript "On memory"]. Passau, Germany: Passavia Universitätsverlag.

Erikson, E. H. (1968). *Identity: Youth and crisis.* Oxford, England: Norton & Co.

Feldman, C., Bruner, J., Kalmar, D., & Renderer, B. (1993). Plot, plight, and dramatism: Interpretation at three ages. *Human Development, 36*, 327–342.

Fivush, R., Bohanek, J. G., & Zaman, W. (2010). Personal and intergenerational narratives in relation to adolescents' well-being. In T. Habermas (Ed.), The development of autobiographical reasoning in adolescence and beyond. *New Directions for Child and Adolescent Development, 131*, 45–57.

Fivush, R., Haden, C. A., & Reese, E. (2006). Elaborating on elaborations: Role of maternal reminiscing style in cognitive and socioemotional development. *Child Development, 77*, 1568–1588.

Frattaroli, J. (2006). Experimental disclosure and its moderators: A meta-analysis. *Psychological Bulletin, 132*, 823–865.

Genereux, R., & McKeough, A. (2007). Developing narrative interpretation: Structural and content analysis. *British Journal of Developmental Psychology, 77*, 849–872.

Gloger-Tippelt, G., Gomille, B., König, L., & Vetter, J. (2002). Attachment representations in 6-year-olds: Related longitudinally to the quality of attachment in infancy and mothers' attachment representations. *Attachment and Human Development, 4*, 318–339.

Habermas, T. (2007). How to tell a life: The development of the cultural concept of biography across the lifespan. *Journal of Cognition and Development, 8*, 1–31.

Habermas, T., & Bluck, S. (2000). Getting a life: The emergence of the life story in adolescence. *Psychological Bulletin, 126*, 748–769.

Habermas, T., & de Silveira, C. (2008). The development of global coherence in life narratives across adolescence: Temporal, causal and thematic aspects. *Developmental Psychology, 44*, 707–721.

Habermas, T., Ehlert-Lerche, S., & de Silveira, C. (2009). The development of the temporal macrostructure of life narratives across adolescence: Beginnings, linear narrative form, and endings. *Journal of Personality, 77*, 527–560.

Habermas, T., Fröhlich, A., & Diel, V. (2009). *Autobiographical reasoning from late childhood to early adulthood: Competence and performance.* Unpublished manuscript, Goethe University: Frankfurt, Germany.

Habermas, T., Negele, A., Arslan, S., & Tavenaux, M. (2008, July). The development of biographical knowledge from late childhood to late adulthood and its influence on life narratives. Paper presented at the XXI International Conference of Psychology, Berlin.

Habermas, T., Negele, A., & Brenneisen-Mayer, F. (in press). "Honey, you're jumping about"—Mothers' scaffolding of their children's and adolescents' life narratives. *Cognitive Development.*

Habermas, T., Ott, L. M., Schubert, M., Schneider, B., & Pate, A. (2008). Stuck in the past: Negative bias, explanatory style, temporal order, and evaluative perspectives in life narratives of clinically depressed individuals. *Depression and Anxiety, 25*, E121–E132.

Habermas, T., & Paha, C. (2001). The development of coherence in adolescents' life narratives. *Narrative Inquiry, 11*, 35–54.

Höpfner, A. (2007). Autobiographical arguments and exemplifications in the AAI of securely and insecurely attached young women. Unpublished diploma thesis, Goethe University, Frankfurt, Germany.

Larsen, R., & Hansen, D. (2005). The development of strategic thinking: Learning to impact human systems in a youth activism program. *Human Development, 48,* 327–349.

Linde, C. (1993). *Life stories.* New York: Oxford University Press.

Lodi-Smith, J., Geise, A. C., Roberts, B. W., & Robins, R. W. (2009). Narrating personality change. *Journal of Personality and Social Psychology, 96,* 679–689.

Mackavey, W. R., Malley, J., & Stewart, A. J. (1991). Remembering autobiographically consequential experiences: Content analysis of psychologists' accounts of their lives. *Psychology and Aging, 6,* 50–59.

Main, M., Kaplan, N., & Cassidy, J. (1985). Security in infancy, childhood, and attachment: A move to the level of representation. In I. Bretherton & E. Waters (Eds.), Growing points of attachment research. *Monographs of the Society for Research in Child Development, 50*(1–2), 66–104.

Mar, R., & Oatley, K. (2008). The function of fiction is the abstraction and simulation of social experience. *Perspectives on Psychological Science, 3,* 173–192.

Mar, R. A., Peskin, J., & Fong, K. (2010). Literary arts and the development of the life story. In T. Habermas (Ed.), The development of autobiographical reasoning in adolescence and beyond. *New Directions for Child and Adolescent Development, 131,* 73–84.

McCabe, A., Capron, E., & Peterson, C. (1991). The voice of experience: The recall of early childhood and adolescent memories by young adults: In A. McCabe & C. Peterson (Eds.), *Developing narrative structure* (pp. 137–173). Hillsdale, NJ: Erlbaum.

McKeough, A., & Genereux, R. (2003). Transformation in narrative thought during adolescence: The structure and content of story composition. *Journal of Educational Psychology, 95,* 537–552.

McKeough, A., & Malcolm, J. (2010). Stories of family, stories of self. In T. Habermas (Ed.), The development of autobiographical reasoning in adolescence and beyond. *New Directions for Child and Adolescent Development, 131,* 59–71.

McLean, K. C. (2008). Stories of the young and the old: Personal continuity and narrative identity. *Developmental Psychology, 44,* 254–264.

McLean, K. C., & Mansfield, C. D. (2010). To reason or not to reason: Is autobiographical reasoning always beneficial? In T. Habermas (Ed.), The development of autobiographical reasoning in adolescence and beyond. *New Directions for Child and Adolescent Development, 131,* 85–97.

McLean, K. C., & Thorne, A. (2003). Late adolescents' self-defining memories about relationships. *Developmental Psychology, 39,* 635–645.

Neisser, U. (Ed.). (1982). *Memory observed: Remembering in natural contexts.* San Francisco: Freeman.

Nelson, K., & Gruendel, J. (1981). Generalized event representations: Basic building blocks of cognitive development. In M. E. Lamb & A. L. Brown (Eds.), *Advances in developmental psychology* (Vol. 1, pp. 31–158). Hillsdale, NJ: Erlbaum.

Neugarten, B. L., Moore, J. W., & Lowe, K. C. (1965). Age norms, age constraints, and adult socialization. *American Journal of Sociology, 70,* 710–717.

Pasupathi, M., & Mansour, E. (2006). Adult age differences in autobiographical reasoning in narratives. *Developmental Psychology, 42,* 798–808.

Pasupathi, M., Mansour, E., & Brubaker, J. (2007). Developing a life story: Constructing relations between self and experience in autobiographical narratives. *Human Development, 50,* 85–110.

Pasupathi, M., & Weeks, T. L. (2010). Integrating self and experience in narrative as a route to adolescent identity development. In T. Habermas (Ed.), The development of autobiographical reasoning in adolescence and beyond. *New Directions for Child and Adolescent Development, 131,* 31–43.

Pasupathi, M., Weeks, T., & Rice, C. (2006). Reflecting on life: Remembering as a major process in adult development. *Journal of Language and Social Psychology, 25,* 244–263.

Pennebaker, J. W., Mayne, T. J., & Francis, M. E. (1997). Linguistic predictors of adaptive bereavement. *Journal of Personality and Social Psychology, 72,* 863–871.

Peterson, C., & McCabe, A. (1994). A social interactionist account of developing decontextualized narrative skill. *Developmental Psychology, 30,* 937–948.

Piaget, J. (1924). *Judgement and reasoning in the child.* New York: Harcourt.

Rubin, D. C. (Ed.). (1986). *Autobiographical memory.* Cambridge, England: Cambridge University Press.

Rubin, D. C., Berntsen, D., & Hutson, M. (2009). The normative and the personal life: Individual differences in life scripts and life story events among USA and Danish undergraduates. *Memory, 17,* 54–68.

Rubin, D. C., & Greenberg, D. L. (2003). The role of narrative in recollection: A view from cognitive psychology and neuropsychology. In G. D. Fireman, T. E. McVay, & O. J. Flanagan (Eds.), *Narrative and consciousness: Literature, psychology, and the brain* (pp. 53–85). New York: Oxford University Press.

Schafer, R. (1983). *The analytic attitude.* New York: Basic Books.

Selman, R. (1980). *The development of social understanding.* New York: Academic Press.

Staudinger, U. M. (2001). Life reflection: A social-cognitive analysis of life review. *Review of General Psychology, 5,* 148–160.

Tonkin, E. (1992). *Narrating our past.* Cambridge, England: Cambridge University Press.

Treynor, W., Gonzalez, R., & Nolen-Hoeksema, S. (2003). Rumination reconsidered: A psychometric analysis. *Cognitive Therapy and Research, 27,* 247–259.

Wang, Q. (2004). The emergence of cultural self-constructs: Autobiographical memory and self-description in European American and Chinese children. *Developmental Psychology, 40,* 3–15.

Webster, J. D. (1993). Construction and validation of the Reminiscence Functions Scale. *Journals of Gerontology, 48,* 256–262.

TILMANN HABERMAS is a professor of psychoanalysis at Goethe University, Frankfurt am Main, Germany.

Bohn, A. (2010). Normative ideas of life and autobiographical reasoning in life narratives. In T. Habermas (Ed.), The development of autobiographical reasoning in adolescence and beyond. New Directions for Child and Adolescent Development, 131, 19–30.

2

Normative Ideas of Life and Autobiographical Reasoning in Life Narratives

Annette Bohn

Abstract

Autobiographical reasoning is closely related to the development of normative ideas about life as measured by the cultural life script. The acquisition of a life script is an important prerequisite for autobiographical reasoning because children learn through the life script which events are expected to go into their life story, and when to expect certain events in life. Thus, the cultural life script not only helps organize autobiographical memories, but it also guides expectations for our future life stories. Therefore, the cultural life script should be considered the overarching principle of organizing autobiographical memories across the lifespan. © Wiley Periodicals, Inc.

This research was supported by post doc grant no. 495952 from the Danish Research Council for Culture and Communication. I would like to thank Dorthe Berntsen, Amanda Miles, Hildur Finburgadottir, and Anne Scharling Rasmussen for helpful comments on this manuscript.

NEW DIRECTIONS FOR CHILD AND ADOLESCENT DEVELOPMENT, no. 131, Spring 2011 © Wiley Periodicals, Inc.
Published online in Wiley Online Library (wileyonlinelibrary.com). • DOI: 10.1002/cd.286

> When I had just learned how to walk and I had my tongue out
> and then I fell and my tongue was bitten in half, so I had to go
> to the hospital, and then the day I came home I did not like to
> use my pacifier any more and I still have a scar.
>
> Frederik, Nine Years Old

Why start a chapter on normative ideas of life and autobiographical reasoning in life narratives with a young boy's account of a negative experience from his past? The answer is that this is not simply the boy's memory of a negative event, but his life story, according to himself. It was produced in response to the task of writing his life story, with explicit instructions to write about "what has happened in your life since you were born and up to now" (Bohn & Berntsen, 2008, p. 1139).

The story conveys information, is easy to follow, and temporally coherent. It can be considered a reasonably coherent narrative of an autobiographical event for a nine-year-old boy. However, the story cannot be called a coherent life story: It reports a single, surely dramatic, incident from the life of this boy, but it conveys nothing about his life from birth until now. Why did he not write his life story, as he had been asked to? In this chapter, I will argue that he lacks the ability of autobiographical reasoning, i.e., the ability to create coherence between remembered autobiographical events, and thus, to turn them into a meaningful life story (Habermas & Bluck, 2000). Further, I will argue that the ability of autobiographical reasoning is closely related to the development of normative ideas about life as measured by the cultural life script (Berntsen & Rubin, 2002, 2004; Rubin & Berntsen, 2003), and that the cultural life script should be considered the overarching organizational principle of autobiographical memories across the lifespan.

Researchers on autobiographical memory have generally emphasized the cultural component playing a role in the formation of both autobiographical memory (see Nelson & Fivush, 2004 for an overview) and life narratives. For example, Reese and Fivush (2008) proposed that the development of autobiographical memory from the beginning is affected by the social and cultural context surrounding the child. Life narratives are thought to be formed by individuals in close interaction with their social and cultural environments (e.g., Habermas & Bluck, 2000; Habermas & Paha, 2001; McAdams, 2001). McAdams defines life stories as "psychosocial constructions, co-authored by the person himself or herself and the cultural context within which that person's life is embedded and given meaning" (McAdams, 2001, p. 100). Thus, life narratives are made up of autobiographical memories that are selected and combined by the individual through the process of autobiographical reasoning to form a coherent personal narrative in the framework of a given cultural context. From this definition of life narratives, two questions are relevant: How do children learn to tell a life story that is personal and at the same time adheres to a culturally defined framework? And how can this cultural framework be measured empirically?

Life Story Coherence

To discuss the influence of cultural norms on the ability to engage in autobiographical reasoning and thus, to tell a coherent life story, the concept of life story coherence needs to be described. Following Habermas and Bluck (2000), a coherent life story is based on four different kinds of coherence. Agreeing with the definition of life narratives as personal narratives within a given cultural framework, Habermas and Bluck describe three types of linguistic or narrative coherence, and one type of cultural coherence called the cultural concept of biography. The three types of narrative coherence are temporal, thematic, and causal coherence. In a coherent life narrative, the temporal sequence of events needs to be respected, i.e., it would be incoherent to mention a job promotion before mentioning getting a job. Thematic coherence refers to the ability to create overarching themes in a narrative and to establish thematic similarities between various (life) events. Through causal coherence, one adds reason and meaning to a life narrative. Causal coherence is necessary to explain how one has become the person that one is. Cultural coherence is specific to the life story and is "used to form a basic, skeletal life narrative consisting of an ordered sequence of culturally defined, major life events" (Habermas & Bluck, 2000, p. 750). The cultural concept of biography is the background and backbone on which the individual life narrative is built. A life narrative should explain—if necessary—deviations from the culturally agreed upon expected life course. Habermas (2006, 2007) has since broadened the definition of the cultural concept of biography to not only include the temporal order in which major life events should occur, but also criteria such as the appropriate beginning and ending of life stories, the handling of less-well-remembered events, and the goal of telling one's life story.

Together, these four types of coherences are involved in the process of autobiographical reasoning, which eventually leads to the establishment of a life story schema (Bluck & Habermas, 2000), which again is used for autobiographical reasoning. Whereas the three types of linguistic coherence can be measured within a life narrative (Habermas & de Silveira, 2008; Habermas & Paha, 2001), only some aspects of the cultural concept of biography can be measured, for example, by looking at the development of beginnings and endings of life stories (Habermas, Ehlert-Lerche, & de Silveira, 2009). A more direct way to measure those aspects of the cultural concept of biography concerned with the temporal order of major life events is the cultural life script, introduced by Berntsen and Rubin (2002, 2004; Rubin & Berntsen, 2003). The cultural life script is the overarching cognitive structure that has been shown to organize life story recall (Collins, Pillemer, Ivcevic, & Gooze, 2007; Glück & Bluck, 2007; Rubin, Berntsen, & Hutson, 2009; Thomsen & Berntsen, 2008; for a more detailed description of these studies, see Bohn, in press), and to be a prerequisite of the development of global life story coherence (Bohn & Berntsen, 2008).

The Cultural Life Script

The cultural life script combines the concept of story scripts (Schank & Abelson, 1977) with the idea of an age segmentation of the lifespan and culturally sanctioned age norms for salient life events (for an overview, see Berntsen & Rubin, 2002, 2004; Neugarten, Moore, & Lowe, 1965). However, cultural life scripts are different in two important ways from story scripts and research on age norms. First, life scripts are not learned by experiencing an event (as one learns the script for eating at a restaurant by eating repeatedly at a restaurant, according to Schank and Abelson, 1977). Rather, life scripts are semantic knowledge learned within one's culture. Second, measures of cultural life scripts are attempted to be free of researcher bias because participants are not asked to rate lists of events pre-chosen by the researcher on salience and age norms, in contrast to what has been done most frequently in research on age norms. Instead, life scripts are measured by asking participants to imagine a newborn child of their own gender in their own culture and to list the most important life events that they think will happen in the newborn's life, as well as to estimate at what age the newborn will experience these events. Therefore, the outcome of the life script task is an empirical measure of the type of life events that different populations in different cultures consider important in life. This makes the life script task an ideal way to measure both the notion of cultural life scripts as well as the related notion of the cultural concept of biography because the instructions for the life script task make this measure at the same time (relatively) bias-free and culture-sensitive.

A cultural life script consists of a series of culturally important transitional events that are expected to take place in a specific order in specific time slots in a prototypical life course within a given culture. The life script is conceptually different from the life story. Life stories are made up of autobiographical memories as they are remembered, reconstructed, and combined by an individual. Cultural life scripts consist of semantic knowledge that is learned detached from personal experience, i.e., young people are able to nominate such events as "getting married" or "retirement" as life script events, even though they have not experienced these events themselves. Life scripts refer to the culturally shared representations of an idealized life. A life script can be described as a series of predominantly positive important transitional events that are expected to happen in a certain order (e.g., "getting married" before "having children"), whereas the order of life story events is dictated by the life a person has lived (e.g., a single teenage mother who gets married later in life). In addition, in a person's life, certain life script events might be "missing"; for example, a person might have remained single. Still, people would be expected to report reasons for the missing life script event "getting married" in their life story because "missing" an event is a deviation from the life script. Each event is allocated a specific time slot in the life course, referring to the age at which the event is normatively expected to take place (e.g., "getting married" around age twenty-seven), while in an individual life, the timing of such life events can be "off," and therefore might need to be accounted for in the personal life story (e.g., "we got married when we were twenty-one because we just knew we would always stay together").

The cultural life script being semantic knowledge has implications not only for the organization of our past life story, but also for the expectations concerning our future life story. With the acquisition of the cultural life script, children not only acquire a template for the organization of their life story as lived until now, but they also acquire a template for what to expect for their future lives within their culture. Empirical findings support this strong future dimension of the cultural life script. Berntsen and Jacobsen (2008) found that when imagining future events, the number of events mapping onto the cultural life script increased with the distance of years the events were imagined to be from the present—participants seemed to rely on their life script knowledge when imagining events farther into the future. In another study, we found that when participants were asked to recall past or to imagine future important events, the majority (71 percent) of all events recalled or imagined were life script events. However, when participants were asked to remember or imagine events to cue words, only few of the recalled or imagined events (20–25 percent) mapped onto the life script. Importantly, also in this study the relation between temporal distance and frequency of life script events was found for all types of events (Berntsen & Bohn, in press). Other studies have shown that when people are asked to nominate important past life events or to think about possible future life events, people tend to nominate events agreeing with the cultural life script (for an overview, see Bohn, in press). Thus, when relating past and future important events to their current selves and identity (a form of autobiographical reasoning), adults use the cultural life script as a frame of reference. Considering the central role the life script plays when adults engage in autobiographical reasoning, it is important to trace the development of this concept in childhood and to tease apart the role of the narrative types of life story coherence (temporal, thematic, and causal) from the role that the concept of cultural biography plays for the development of a coherent life story.

Methodologically, the concept of the cultural life script makes it possible to measure the cultural concept of biography separately from the life story. The advantage of this method is that it makes it possible to disentangle the development of "ordinary" narrative coherence (temporal, causal, and thematic) from the development of life story coherence, which by definition includes cultural coherence whereas other narratives do not (Habermas & Bluck, 2000).

Dorthe Berntsen and I conducted a study concerned with the development of these two different types of coherences (Bohn & Berntsen, 2008; Berntsen & Bohn, 2009). Frederik's life story in the beginning of this chapter stems from this study. In the following paragraphs, I will briefly describe our study and its results. The main purpose of the study was to investigate at what age children develop an adult-like, normative life script, at what age children develop a coherent life story, and whether the acquisition of a cultural life script is related to the development of life story coherence. Participants in our study were 120 Danish school-aged children with a middle-class background, consisting of three groups of children with an average age of nine and a half years, twelve years, and fourteen and a half years. The groups consisted of approximately the same number of boys and girls. The children were asked (1) to write a story about their recent fall vacation, (2) to write their life story, and (3) to generate a cultural life script. An adult norm for the life script was established by collecting cultural life scripts from 111 young adults with a mean age of twenty-eight years.

Data collection took place during regular school lessons over a period of three weeks. The fall vacation stories were collected to establish a baseline measure of narrative coherence in single event stories. The rationale behind collecting a baseline story was that, if indeed cultural coherence is specific to the life story, as hypothesized by Habermas and Bluck (2000), then the acquisition of an adult-like life script should play much less of a role for the development of story coherence in the single event stories.

Just like Habermas and de Silviera (2008) in their study on oral life stories, we found that overall life story coherence increased significantly with age. Children became better across age groups at beginning and ending their life stories in a more normative way, i.e., older children were more likely to begin their life stories with their birth, and to finish their life stories in the present. Including normative beginnings and endings in a life story can be interpreted as a sign of cultural coherence (Habermas et al., 2009). In line with this, we found that children whose life narratives had a more mature temporal macrostructure (i.e., who started their life stories with or even before their birth, and ended it in the present) had more normative life scripts ($r = .25$, $p < 0.01$ for beginning of life stories and $r = .35$, $p < 0.001$ for the ending of life stories, controlled for age).

We also found that the narrative coherence of the fall vacation stories improved with age. However, interestingly, we found no relationship between the children's ability to create a coherent story of a single event and their ability to create a coherent life story. Further, even when statistically controlling for the age of our participants, we found that there was a significant correlation between how normative or adult-like the cultural life scripts of the children were and their ability to produce a coherent life story. On the other hand, there was no relationship between the normativity of the children's life scripts and their ability to tell a coherent story about a single autobiographical event. The results suggest that the development of narrative coherence and global life story coherence follow different pathways, and it provides evidence for Habermas's and Bluck's (2000) claim that the cultural concept of biography as measured by the cultural life script is specific to the ability to engage in autobiographical reasoning and thus, to produce a coherent life story.

The case of the boy Frederik illustrates our findings. Frederik was able to tell a reasonably coherent story from his fall vacation, but he was not able to write a coherent life story. Importantly, Frederik generated a life script that deviated extremely from the adult norm (see Table 2.1; for other examples of children's life scripts, see Berntsen & Bohn, 2009). The results from our study suggest that children acquire a cultural life script across childhood and into adolescence.

These findings agree with findings from a study on the development of age norms for salient life events (Habermas, 2007). However, both studies were cross-sectional. To extend our findings, I have begun to collect longitudinal data on the children who were in third grade at the time of the study reported here, and who are in sixth grade today, including Frederik. Though very preliminary and qualitative, Frederik's current life script and life story can highlight the interplay between the cultural life script, autobiographical reasoning, and the development of the narrative coherences. To recapitulate, in third grade Frederik produced an extremely non-normative life script (Table 2.1). His life script contained only two events that are also part of the adult life script (retirement and death), but otherwise it consisted of idiosyncratic events. Clearly, he had not yet acquired a life script that could help him anchor the events of his own life within a culturally expected life course. Consequently, he wrote a life story that described only a single, very memorable episode from his life: an accident at a very young age that involved a visit to the hospital. Table 2.1 also presents Frederik's current life script. The following is Frederik's current life story.

> It all started when I was born at the University Hospital. When I was two months old, my mother went to something where she met another mother who had had a baby in the same room as she had. She was called Lene and her child was named Bo. Me and Bo have gone to daycare and kindergarten together and go in the same grade now.

> We are best friends now, and have been thinking that we will go on skiing holiday together next year. He'll be snowboarding and I'll be skiing.

Table 2.1. Example of the Development of the Cultural Life Script from Age Nine to Twelve

Frederik's Life Script at Age Nine	Age at Event
He is ill	0
He becomes famous	1
He moves to England	10
And then he moves to Denmark again	20
And he's rich	30
He becomes famous	35
And he becomes a famous football player	15
And then he retires	36
And then he dies	70

Frederik's Life Script at Age Twelve	Age at Event
Starting school	7
High school	21
He gets good grades in ninth grade	15
He makes new friends	20
He begins drinking and partying	16
Gets a job	21
Wife and children	26
He gets a career	30
Time of retirement	60
Death	100

When I just had learned to walk, I ran with my tongue out of my mouth and fell. When I fell, I bit my tongue in half and when I was at the emergency room, the doctor said she could not sew a tongue because a tongue is a muscle. She also said that the only way it could grow together again was by leaving it in peace. From that day, I have never used a pacifier again.

When I started in kindergarten, I coughed and could not breathe so we went to the doctor again. We were told that I had asthma and I was going to a special doctor every three months. I still have asthma but do not suffer from it because I've got the right medicine.

At age twelve, Frederik's life story has become more of a life story. He now begins his life story with his birth, and his place of birth is related to the meeting of his first and best friend, Bo. Frederik includes life script-related activities such as going to day care, kindergarten, and school in his life story. He tells about the time that he learned about his chronic disease, and he ends his life story in the present with something that resembles what Habermas et al. (2009) called a global evaluation: He relates his disease to his present self and evaluates the situation (positively). Clearly,

Frederik has developed the ability of autobiographical reasoning. He relates events from his past to his present self (how he met his best friend Bo, and that they are still friends), and even envisions plans for activities with his friend that extend beyond the next few months (going on a ski vacation together "next year").

If the acquisition of an adult-like cultural life script is related to the development of autobiographical reasoning, as argued in this chapter, then Frederik's current life script should mirror this by being more normative than his life script at the age of nine. An inspection of his current life script presented in Table 2.1 supports this hypothesis. The majority of events in his life script are now events that are also part of the adult cultural life script. For most events, his age estimates are within the normative timeslot. However, his life script still lacks complete chronological order, i.e., events are not (yet) mentioned in the order at which he expects them to occur. This jumping back and forth in time is also apparent in Frederik's life story. After he has told the reader about his birth and meeting his best friend, and about their joint experiences and plans for the future, he returns to an incident that happened to him when he must have been approximately one year old ("when I just had started to walk").

This part of Frederik's life story is interesting for various reasons. First, his life story at age nine consisted solely of this incident. In agreement with theory (Habermas & Bluck, 2000; Berntsen & Rubin, 2002, 2004), Frederik includes an important event from his life that is deviant from the cultural life script in his life story. Of course, it could be that Frederik included this incident in his new life story because he remembered having written about it three years earlier. Other (preliminary) data from the longitudinal study speak against this: There is some evidence that children who wrote single event life stories at age nine only include these events in their current life story if they had been traumatic (such as getting lost on the beach or getting hit by a car). Children who wrote single-event life stories about mundane events (like going on vacation or shopping) at age nine did not write about these events again at age twelve. But Frederik's new description of his accident as a (presumably) one-year-old is also intriguing when seen in relation to other cultural and social influences on the life story beyond the cultural life script. Clearly, his description of the accident as a twelve-year-old mirrors that this accident must have been talked about repeatedly in the family. Possibly, his accident might have been a topic of dinnertime narratives, as described by Fivush, Bohanek, and Zaman (Chapter Four). Frederik's current description of the incident is about 40 percent longer than his original account. He now includes information that he could not possibly remember from the original event (the physician's statement that the tongue is a muscle and can only heal by leaving it alone). This new information seems to be a combination of things he has heard his family tell about the event, and things that he might have learned in school (that the tongue is a muscle). The development of Frederik's report about his accident illustrates nicely, I think, that autobiographical memory and life stories are developed through the interplay between the individual and social and cultural surroundings, especially when considering Frederik's extremely young age at the time of the accident. It might well be that he doesn't actually have a memory of the event, but has heard stories about this accident so often that he has made his family's memory into his own.

Though based on preliminary qualitative results, Frederik's case supports the claim that children need to acquire a fairly normative cultural life script to engage in autobiographical reasoning. It seems that children need to have an idea about how a typical life is ideally lived within their culture to select events from their own life that can be woven into a coherent life story. Further, the life script teaches children what to expect for their future life within their culture. It is this anchoring of the individual in his or her culture that goes beyond the two prerequisites of autobiographical reasoning (being able to narrate a story and having a sense of self) identified by researchers (Habermas & Bluck, 2000; Pasupathi & Mansour, 2006) and makes autobiographical reasoning possible. As pointed out by many researchers on autobiographical memory (e.g., Nelson & Fivush, 2004), the development of autobiographical memory is closely interwoven with social and cultural interactions. In a life narrative perspective, this means that life stories cannot be told without the narrator being able to anchor his or her story within his or her culture. It is the cultural life script that provides the narrator with a guideline as to which events to include in the life story, and, if necessary, to explain the deviations from the life script in this story—both concerning the type of events narrated and the timing of the events.

Theoretical Implications

The cultural life script is semantic knowledge about an entire life span within a culture that is acquired across childhood and adolescence. Thus, the knowledge of the life script includes a strong future dimension. This differentiates the cultural life script from other models on the organization of autobiographical memory, like the life story schema that is formed "as a residue of repeated speaking, thinking, and reasoning about the events of one's past through which events are related to one another and to the self" (Habermas & Bluck, 2000, p.127).

In the life story schema, the cultural concept of biography is seen as one type of life story coherence on the same level as the three types of linguistic coherence. However, as the results presented in this chapter suggest, the acquisition of the cultural life script is an important prerequisite for the ability of autobiographical reasoning because it facilitates the connection between the self and the culture beyond the individual life story.

Further, children and adolescents are able to tell temporally, causally, and thematically coherent stories of single events independent of their life script abilities. However, their ability to tell a coherent *life* story is not independent of their life script abilities. Therefore, it seems, the cultural life script is the frame that holds life stories together: Cultural life scripts teach children which events are expected to be in their life story, and when to expect certain events in life. It seems that the life script provides the "plot" of one's life story. Having a plot makes it much easier to tell a coherent life story, where one thing leads to another, and events are neatly tied together through the process of autobiographical reasoning. Therefore, the cultural life script should be considered the overarching organizational principle of autobiographical memories across the lifespan.

References

Berntsen, D., & Bohn, A. (2009). Cultural life scripts and individual life stories. In P. Boyer & J. V. Wertsch (Eds.), *Memory in mind and culture* (pp. 62–82). Cambridge, England: Cambridge University Press.

Berntsen, D., & Bohn, A. (in press). Remembering and forecasting: The relation between autobiographical memory and episodic future thinking. *Memory and Cognition.*

Berntsen, D., & Jacobsen, A. S. (2008). Involuntary (spontaneous) mental time travel into the past and future. *Consciousness and Cognition, 17,* 1093–1104.

Berntsen, D., & Rubin, D. C. (2002). Emotionally charged autobiographical memories across the life span: The recall of happy, sad, traumatic, and involuntary memories. *Psychology and Aging, 17,* 636–652.

Berntsen, D., & Rubin, D. C. (2004). Cultural life scripts structure recall from autobiographical memory. *Memory & Cognition, 32,* 427–442.

Bohn, A. (in press). Generational differences in cultural life scripts and life story memories of younger and older adults. *Applied Cognitive Psychology.*

Bohn, A., & Berntsen, D. (2008). Life story development in childhood: The development of life story abilities and the acquisition of cultural life scripts from late middle childhood to adolescence. *Developmental Psychology, 44,* 1135–1142.

Collins, K. A., Pillemer, D. B., Ivcevic, Z., & Gooze, R. A. (2007). Cultural scripts guide recall of intensely positive life events. *Memory & Cognition, 35 (4),* 651–659.

Fivush, R., Bohanek, J. G., & Zaman, W. (2010). Personal and intergenerational narratives in relation to adolescents' well-being. In Habermas, T. (Ed.), The development of autobiographical reasoning in adolescence and beyond. *New Directions for Child and Adolescent Development, 131,* 45–57.

Glück, J., & Bluck, S. (2007). Looking back across the lifespan: A life story account of the reminiscence bump. *Memory and Cognition, 35,* 1928–1935.

Habermas, T. (2006). Kann ich auch ganz, ganz am Anfang anfangen? Wie Jugendliche lernen, Lebenserzählungen zu eröffnen und beenden [Can I start at the very beginning? How adolescents learn how to begin and end life narratives]. In H. Welzer & H. J. Markowitsch (Eds.), Warum Menschen sich erinnern: Fortschritte der interdisziplinären Gedächtnisforschung [Why people remember: Advances in interdisciplinary memory research], (pp. 256–275). Stuttgart, Germany: Klett-Cotta.

Habermas, T. (2007). How to tell a life: The development of the cultural concept of biography. *Journal of Cognition and Development, 8(1),* 1–31.

Habermas, T., & Bluck, S. (2000). Getting a life: The emergence of the life story in adolescence. *Psychological Bulletin, 126*(5), 748–769.

Habermas, T., & de Silveira, C. (2008). The development of global coherence in life narratives across adolescence: Temporal, causal and thematic aspects. *Developmental Psychology, 44*(3), 707–721.

Habermas, T., Ehlert-Lerche, S., & de Silveira, C. (2009). The development of the temporal macrostructure of life narratives across adolescence: Beginnings, linear narrative form, and endings. *Journal of Personality, 77,* 527–560.

Habermas, T., & Paha, C. (2001). The development of coherence in adolescents' life narratives. *Narrative Inquiry, 11*(1), 35–54.

McAdams, D. P. (2001). The psychology of life stories. *Review of General Psychology, 5,* 100–122.

Nelson, K., & Fivush, R. (2004). The emergence of autobiographical memory: A social cultural developmental theory. *Psychological Review, 111*(2), 486–511.

Neugarten, B. L., Moore, J. W., & Lowe, J. C. (1965). Age norms, age constraints, and adult socialization. *The American Journal of Sociology, 70,* 710–717.

Pasupathi, M., & Mansour, E. (2006). Adult age differences in autobiographical reasoning in narratives. *Developmental Psychology, 42,* 798–808.

Reese, E., & Fivush, R. (2008). The development of collective remembering. *Memory, 16*(3), 201–212.

Rubin, D. C., & Berntsen, D. (2003). Life scripts help to maintain autobiographical memories of highly positive, but not highly negative, events. *Memory & Cognition, 31,* 1–14.

Rubin, D. C., Berntsen, D., & Hutson, M. (2009). The normative and the personal life: Individual differences in life scripts and life story events among USA and Danish undergraduates. *Memory, 17,* 54–68.

Schank, R. C., & Abelson, R. P. (1977). Scripts, plans, and knowledge. In P. N. Johnson-Laird & P. C. Watson (Eds.), *Thinking. Readings in cognitive science* (pp. 421–435). Cambridge, England: Cambridge University Press.

Thomsen, D., & Berntsen, D. (2008). The cultural life script and life story chapters contribute to the reminiscence bump. *Memory, 16* (4), 420–435.

ANNETTE BOHN *is an assistant professor of cognitive psychology at the Center for Autobiographical Memory Research (Con Amore) at Aarhus University, Aarhus, Denmark.*

Pasupathi, M., & Weeks, T. L. (2010). Integrating self and experience in narrative as a route to adolescent identity construction. In T. Habermas (Ed.), The development of autobiographical reasoning in adolescence and beyond. *New Directions for Child and Adolescent Development, 131*, 31–43.

3

Integrating Self and Experience in Narrative as a Route to Adolescent Identity Construction

Monisha Pasupathi, Trisha L. Weeks

Abstract

The authors outline the concept of self-event relations and propose that adolescents accomplish narrative identity construction in part by building relations between self and experience as they tell stories about their lives. They outline different types of self-event relations and consider how they contribute to building a sense of identity. They then examine the likely developmental trajectory of self-event relations from childhood through adolescence. Finally, the authors consider the importance of conversational narration in allowing expert adults, especially parents, to help adolescents acquire skills in constructing self-event relations. © Wiley Periodicals, Inc.

NEW DIRECTIONS FOR CHILD AND ADOLESCENT DEVELOPMENT, no. 131, Spring 2011 © Wiley Periodicals, Inc.
Published online in Wiley Online Library (wileyonlinelibrary.com). • DOI: 10.1002/cd.287

One of the central problems for adolescents and young adults is to resolve the challenge of seeing themselves as the same person over time, and to build a sense of themselves that integrates their past and present, and connects to an emerging future. This challenge is typically labeled constructing an identity. In this chapter, we first note how some distinct approaches to identity in adolescence have converged on the importance of narratives for identity construction. Autobiographical reasoning within narratives may be of particular importance for identity, and we outline how self-event relations, one type of autobiographical reasoning, can provide for a sense of identity. We then consider the developmental trajectory of self-event relations, which appear to emerge during adolescence. Finally, we turn to the role of dialogue with others, especially adults, in helping adolescents to construct meaningful connections between their sense of self and their experiences.

The concept of identity has a long philosophical and psychological history (Chandler, Lalonde, Sokol, & Hallett, 2003; Erikson & Erikson, 1997; Locke, 1996; McAdams, 1996; Schectman, 2003). From the standpoint of some philosophers (e.g., Locke, 1996; Schectman, 2003), identity is fundamentally about sameness over time—the notion that two objects are the same, or, in relation to psychological concepts of identity, that one has remained the same person over time. From a psychological standpoint, however, just what constitutes equivalence over time is not quite clear. In what ways is the young mother and wife the same person as the partying adolescent? How is that partying, wild, independent adolescent like the good little schoolgirl? Given the changing capabilities and characteristics of the developing person, a sense of identity must be constructed by individuals rather than taken for granted. Further, times of rapid developmental and social-contextual change can pose particular challenges to the person engaged in constructing a sense of identity, and adolescence and early adulthood represent such a time.

It is not surprising, then, that adolescence and early adulthood have been highlighted as the key phase for the development of identity by many psychologists (Erikson & Erikson, 1997; Harter, 1998; McAdams & Cox, in press; McLean, Pasupathi, & Pals, 2007). Importantly, however, this emphasis on identity development in adolescence and early adulthood can be seen as having two distinct foci. One emphasizes the process and contents of identity—exploring distinct roles and ideologies, and committing to some (Erikson & Erikson, 1997; Marcia, 1966). The other is on the experience of, and belief in, one's continuity in identity over time—the sense of being the same person through time (Chandler et al., 2003; Erikson & Erikson, 1997; McAdams & Cox, in press). Identity in the form of roles and commitments can provide a sense of continuity in identity over time, as roles and commitments frame past actions and serve to guide future ones in ways that promote continuity. However, direct explorations of how people come to view themselves as the same person over time are relatively sparse.

The most directly related findings are those of Chandler and colleagues, who have examined developmental changes in the way children and adolescents can reason about continuity of identity over time (Chandler et al., 2003). They document a progressive, age-related increase in the sophistication with which people can resolve apparent discontinuities in the identities of story characters, as well as in their own identity over time. They also found two distinct types of approaches, which they term essentialist and narrativist approaches. Essentialist strategies emphasize ways in which the person has maintained the same attributes over time, although they vary in sophistication and abstraction across development. Narrativist strategies are more complex, and entail an appeal to the idea that one individual has experienced all the events in that person's life as the basis for continuity in identity. At a simple level, essentialist strategies say, "I'm the same because I have always been sociable," and narrativist strategies say, "I'm the same because I am the person to whom all these things have happened." Interestingly, McAdams (1996) has similarly focused on the way that the story of one's life is one way to conceive of identity. That is, in constructing the story of the past, present, and projected future, people necessarily place themselves in the role of an agent who is continuous over time. Moreover, this placement allows for a sense of identity even in the face of substantial change.

Self-Event Connections

Both Chandler and McAdams, though working in different traditions, converge on the notion that narrative can play an important role in the resolution of challenges to identity. However, Chandler's work suggests that not all narratives will resolve challenges to identity with equal effectiveness. In Chandler's work, which is explicitly developmental in its focus, some narratives reflect more sophisticated strategies for establishing identity than others do. The more sophisticated narrative strategies connected stories about the past and present self in maturational or causal ways; the most sophisticated narrative strategies grasped the interpretive quality of those connections. Chandler's work involves explicitly asking participants to explain how they are the same person across time. In contrast, research within the broader narrative identity tradition has examined the way that stories constructed by people about their own lives reflect continuous themes and emotional sequences (McAdams, 1996; McAdams & Cox, in press), or links between self and experience (Habermas & Paha, 1999; Pasupathi, Mansour, & Brubaker, 2007). The latter connections represent elements of levels two and three in Chandler's set of narrative strategies for continuity, in that they link continuity of self to the ways that the present is shaped by the past and can potentially shape the future. They are also a prototypical example of autobiographical reasoning, the focus of this volume.

Types of Self-Event Connections. Looking in more detailed ways at the types of self-event links that people construct in narratives about their lives suggests that adults have a variety of distinctive ways of linking self with events; in our work, we have identified at least six distinct types of self-event relationships that people may build in the context of telling stories about their everyday lives. These strategies are presented in Table 3.1. Some involve stability; others engender change.

Table 3.1. Self-Event Relations

Self-Event Relation	Brief Definition and Examples
Stability-maintaining	
Explanatory	An aspect of self *explains* why an event occurred
	"Because I am a good cook, she invited me to cater her event."
Illustrative	An aspect of self is *illustrated* by an event
	"I'm really outgoing—sometimes too much so. For example, one time I was at a party and just went up to some people and kind of joined them, and later found out they were trying really hard to talk about a private matter."
Dismissal	An event suggests or challenges some aspect of self, but should be *dismissed* as evidence for/against that aspect of self
	"Normally I'm very conscientious about my studies, but this past week I just went out and got drunk right before a test, and I hadn't studied. I was under a lot of stress, and I guess I just wasn't quite my usual self."
Change-engendering	
Causal	The event *causes* a change in my self-views
	"I took my first yoga class, and afterwards I felt like a much more calm and focused person."
Revealing	The event *reveals* a previously unrecognized aspect of my self.
	"After our near-miss accident, I realized that I can maintain a, surprisingly, level of calm under very high pressure—something I didn't know I was capable of."
Unclear effect	
Challenge	The event is described as a *challenge* to an existing self-view, but no resolution is offered in the narrative for how this challenge can be resolved.
	"I am usually someone with very high moral standards, but last week at the party I got very drunk and then drove that way, without calling for a ride, and I put myself and my friends in danger."
Juxtaposition	The event is described *juxtaposed* with a self-related claim but the relationship between event and self is unclear.
	In the midst of a narrative about driving drunk, a teenage girl says "Maybe it will change my lack of spirituality," and then exchanges two conversational turns with her mother regarding her college plans. The relationship between lack of spirituality and the event of driving drunk is unclear.

NEW DIRECTIONS FOR CHILD AND ADOLESCENT DEVELOPMENT • DOI: 10.1002/cd

People may maintain identity by linking experiences to the kind of person they believe themselves to be, either in a causal or illustrative way. Further, people also engage in constructing relations that dismiss challenges to their existing sense of self. However, people also tell stories that articulate the ways in which they have changed, either because events have changed them, or because an experience illuminated previously unrecognized qualities. Note that both stability and change engendering relations create continuity in the self by linking past, present, and sometimes future to one agent.

The above types of self-event relations suggest people have a hunch about the relation between experiences and their sense of self. In other cases, however, people appear to be struggling with the implications of events. Such a struggle is sometimes reflected in narratives that articulate a *challenge* to self-conceptions, but a challenge that is either left unresolved or which is given multiple, somewhat conflicting resolutions. For example, consider the excerpt below, in which a participant was asked to narrate an event that was "not like her." Her narrative, however, explains her behavior as completely consistent with her understanding of herself—and indeed, the italicized text articulates a self-event relation in which her trait (competitiveness) causes her bad behavior. She went on to suggest that something about this event was not like her—namely, that this event suggests she is short-tempered and inconsiderate. Across the entire narrative, the participant expresses a clear challenge to a desired sense of self (considerate, even-tempered), but one in which her narrative can be interpreted as involving incoherent resolutions—to some extent acknowledging that this event is like her.

> This was around two weeks ago at my in-laws house in Bountiful. I told my husband he was being a moron. This occurred during a game of Yahtzee and, *due to my somewhat overly competitive nature, I got a little carried away with myself* (I was doing badly) and John, my husband, offered some advice. I was irritated and fed up with the game and displaced my ill will towards it on innocent John. With an angry look and voice I said, "I don't need advice from a moron like you!"

The example shows a challenge with conflicting resolutions, but often challenges are expressed, but left unresolved (Rice & Pasupathi, in press). *Juxtapositions* are even less clear in their implications—in a *juxtaposition*, self-conceptions are offered in the narrative neighborhood of descriptions of the event, but are not further elaborated.

In adults' everyday narratives, stability-maintaining self-event relations are among the most prevalent (McLean & Pasupathi, in press; Pasupathi & Mansour, 2006; Pasupathi, Mansour, et al., 2007), although this is less often the case when narratives are about turning points or major crises (Pasupathi & Mansour, 2006; Pasupathi, Mansour, et al., 2007).

NEW DIRECTIONS FOR CHILD AND ADOLESCENT DEVELOPMENT • DOI: 10.1002/cd

Further, people clearly adapt their self-event relations to maintain a stable sense of themselves over time, by using dismissals when events challenge the self and explaining or illustrating relations for other events. This emphasis on stability of self-perceptions among educated and largely European American samples is in keeping with Chandler and colleagues' findings on essentialist strategies for constructing continuity of identity (Chandler et al., 2003) and is also consistent with self-verification theory (Swann, 2000).

Development of Self-Event Connections. Developmental work on self-event relations and closely related constructs has generally examined age differences in the prevalence of self-event relationships, and has suggested several dimensions along which developmental changes occur. First, Pasupathi and Mansour (2006) showed age-related increases in the prevalence of self-event relations over adulthood, peaking in middle adulthood (Bluck & Gluck, 2004). McLean and colleagues (McLean, Breen, & Fournier, in press) and Habermas and colleagues (Habermas & de Silveira, 2008) have shown that the prevalence of self-event relations also increases from late childhood through adolescence in U.S. American and German samples. These findings suggest that adolescence is a key age period for constructing self-event relationships, although development continues into middle adulthood.

Some types of self-event connections appear to emerge earlier than others do. For example, Habermas and de Silveira (2008) found that links in which personality explains life events (explain connections) emerged earlier and were more prevalent than relations in which life events explain personality (cause and reveal relations); their category of exemplification, something like the illustrative relation in Table 3.1, also was evident even in eight-year-olds, but increased dramatically with age. These findings suggest that some classes of stability-engendering relations are likely to be available to children earlier than are change-engendering relations (see also Pasupathi & Wainryb, in press).

Existing examinations of the development of self-event relationships have limitations. They are primarily focused on people from cultures that tend to emphasize essentialist perspectives on identity (Chandler et al., 2003). Some types of self-event relationships are rare, and therefore require larger sample sizes to investigate. Existing work has not always focused on exploring self-event relations of different types. Finally, to our knowledge, no work has explicitly tested whether self-event relations do foster a sense of identity with assessments that are independent of narrative. An additional limitation in this work is the extent to which it proceeds from examinations of written or interviewer-elicited narratives. The vast majority of narrative construction is done in conversational contexts, with family and friends. Such dialogue-oriented settings may reveal much about the developmental processes by which self-event relationships are scaffolded by others and ultimately adopted by adolescents themselves.

Self-Event Connections in Conversational Narrations. Dialogue may be particularly important for adolescents to construct self-event relations, given the late developmental emergence of the capacity to build such relationships in their own narratives (Habermas & de Silveira, 2008; McLean et al., 2010; Pasupathi & Wainryb, in press). There is little work on listener contributions to adolescents' self-event connections in narrative, whether in the form of offering their own self-event connections, or in terms of their responses to adolescents' self-conceptions. However, studies emphasizing early childhood (Fivush & Nelson, 2004; Reese, Bird, & Tripp, 2007) and adulthood (McLean et al., 2007; Pasupathi & Mansour, 2006; Pasupathi, Mansour, et al., 2007; Rice & Pasupathi, in press) point to variations in listener responsiveness, which are related to whether listeners provide their own ideas about relations between events and the speaker's identity, and to the way listeners respond to speakers' self-event relations.

Much of this work centers on the concept of responsiveness. Listeners who are responsive pay attention, ask questions and contribute to the narrative, and support the telling of a story, although not necessarily the specific content offered by a narrator. Children whose mothers are highly responsive, and adults whose friends are highly responsive, tell more elaborative and meaning-laden stories to those listeners, and subsequently have more elaborated memories for the experiences they have narrated (Fivush & Nelson, 2004; Pasupathi & Hoyt, 2009). Responsive listening for negative events (Weeks & Pasupathi, in press) and meaning-oriented telling for novel events (Weeks & Pasupathi, in preparation) promotes the integration of those events with the narrator's self concept.

Responsive listeners are necessarily attentive to speakers. However, child research shows that responsive mothers usually combine attentiveness with support or agreement for the child's unique rendering of events, and with expert help with structuring memory (Cleveland & Reese, 2005), suggesting that in addition to attentiveness, these other elements of listener responsiveness warrant attention. Across child and adult developmental work, listeners who are responsive usually express agreement, whether verbally ("Yes, I think so too.") or non-verbally (via nodding, smiling, etc.), and speakers usually see responsive listeners as agreeable (Pasupathi & Hoyt, 2009). Agreement is not a necessary part of responsiveness—sometimes responsiveness can be combined with disagreement and conflict (e.g., Pasupathi, Carstensen, Levenson, & Gottman, 1999; Pasupathi & Hoyt, 2009). However, when speakers and listeners agree about self-event connections, those connections are especially likely to be retained by the speaker over time (McLean & Pasupathi, in press).

Responsive mothers also have expertise about remembering what they can use to support young children's needs in producing a complete autobiographical narrative. In terms of *how to remember*, the gap between mothers' expertise and children's ability diminishes well before adolescence. However, even through middle adolescence, expert help from parents may assist adolescents in constructing self-event connections. In normative settings, mothers and fathers continue to have a greater expertise on some aspects of continuity in their child's lives both because they have access to memories of the child's life and experience prior to the offset of infantile amnesia, and because they may have a longer temporal scope in terms of the child's future. In other words, parents can help even their adult children to link current life experiences with lifelong proclivities, and with future possibilities.

For example, the following dialogue between a seventeen-year-old girl and her mother was collected in a pilot study in our laboratory (Weeks & Pasupathi, 2010); the mother points out her daughter's proclivity to value friendship. She suggests this trait has always been true of her daughter. The mother also highlights the importance of friendship for the girl's future:

> Daughter:…just kind of the friend changes I've been going through…I learned about myself that I have the confidence to go out, go talk to people, go make new friends like Anna…it's something I kind of have to relearn every once in a while just…um, just kind of get used to putting that energy and effort into it.
>
> Mother: Well, and making friends is important to you—
>
> Daughter: Yeah.
>
> Mother:—it's important to you…it was a little bit to Sarah, but it is definitely more important to you than it was to your older sister and, um, having those friends is important to you and you've learned how to branch out. And you also have a lot of compassion for friends, which is a really good thing to have.
>
> Daughter: That's—that's how me and Anna bonded. It was like, you know, I have my John crap and she had trouble with her friends and like—I don't know, it's just when you have something like that in common it's really easy to make friends.
>
> [*Several turns about the development of Sarah's social life omitted*]
>
> Mother: But—it's—it's a really—it's something that you'll use the rest of your life to become a person of kindness and interested in others and to be a positive person. It's—it's something you will use for the rest of your life no matter where you go…no matter what you do by, um, making people feel warm and welcome around you. And by being a loving person, showing kindness, is probably the most important thing—an important way that you can be.

As the above conversation shows, responsive listeners are motivated to help children and adolescents construct their experiences, and to build a sense of identity in relation to those events. The following dialogue

NEW DIRECTIONS FOR CHILD AND ADOLESCENT DEVELOPMENT • DOI: 10.1002/cd

between a fourteen-year-old girl and her mother is about a role the girl recently played in a performance. The mother challenges the girl's assertions about the effect of this experience on her identity.

> Daughter: Okay, um—well the first experience of a negative that um—um, changed how I thought about myself—and it was the Potipher's wife thing…yeah. So it was just weird—having to, like, do that flirtatious kind of attitude, I learned that I'm not like that in any way, shape, or form. And I guess I kind of already knew that, but it just, kind of, made me even more— deep down there I'm not flirtatious.
>
> Mother: Not yet.
>
> Daughter: No, probably never.
>
> Mother: One day you will be.
>
> Daughter: No, I'll always be that awkward one—yeah.
>
> Mother: Why—why do you say it changed you?
>
> Daughter: Well, I just…it helped me step out of my shell a lot more. Like I was living in this little shell and by doing that, it stepped out. And that's why I made the friends that I had in that acting class is because I stepped out of that shell—by being Potipher's wife, helped me with that—yeah.
>
> Mother: I didn't see any big dramatic changes in you from that.
>
> Daughter: Um, okay.
>
> Mother: I mean, I saw you step out of your—I knew it was uncomfortable for you….
>
> Daughter: Yeah.
>
> Mother: I thought it was good for you to experience that.
>
> Daughter: Okay.
>
> Mother: That's what I thought.

In this dialogue, the daughter implies that flirtatiousness is an enduring personality trait, and that she possesses awkwardness in its place. The mother challenges this assumption and implies that flirtatiousness is something one can grow into (and perhaps that awkwardness is something one can grow out of). Unable to win the point with her daughter, the mother then inquires as to why the girl thinks the role of Potipher's wife changed her. The daughter asserts that "getting out of her shell" is a change for her. The mother challenges the claim that the girl has been changed, and then reframes the accomplishment of "stepping out" as a normative, albeit uncomfortable experience. The mother here is both

NEW DIRECTIONS FOR CHILD AND ADOLESCENT DEVELOPMENT • DOI: 10.1002/cd

pushing for growth in terms of skills and experiences ("one day you will be [flirtatious]"; "I thought it was good for you to experience that"), and making an argument for stability in the girl's general identity ("I didn't see any big dramatic changes in you from that.").

Adolescence also entails a shift in the primary audience for personal storytelling, from parents, to friends and romantic partners, and there are also relationship-specific facets of listeners roles. Distinct relational contexts involve listeners with a different set of concerns about the adolescents' identity, with corresponding implications for the dialogical construction of self-event relationships. Because parents have both a long, intimate history and an imagined future with their children, they may serve as an audience that emphasizes stability in the child's identity, perhaps via reconstructing changes as the unfolding of potential, and growth in terms of acquiring skills and experience. Parents may also be more apt than friends are to focus on aspects of events involving the safety or risky behavior of their children. Friends, on the other hand, may be more focused on being supportive of the adolescent's changing self-views, and on promoting exploration of the self.

The disparities between different types of listeners and their motivations can be, from our perspective, a source for the development and exploration of a richer and more complex identity. For example, the juxtaposition quoted in Table 3.1 occurred in dialogue between the adolescent and her mother regarding a drunk driving incident. In the context of that conversational narrative, the meaning of references to herself as "an example" was unclear, and those references were coded as juxtapositions. This adolescent also narrated the drunk driving incident with her best friend (Weeks & Pasupathi, 2010). In that conversation, what had been an unelaborated juxtaposition in the conversation with the mother became much clearer. The narrator had always conceived of herself as setting a moral example to her friends (and been seen similarly by her friends). This self-conception was challenged by the drunk driving incident, in ways that had not yet been resolved by the teen. In conversational narration with her friend, the teen was able to explore this challenge, and the friend offered a resolution that interpreted the incident as congruent with being a good moral example. The mother could not resolve the concern about being an example for her friends because the friends were arguably the only people who could verify this self-view. Moreover, the drunk driving incident was very differently narrated with mother and friend, but in ways that were congruent rather than conflicted, allowing the narrator to fully explore the identity implications of the event across the two contexts.

Conclusion

Identity continuity is emerging as a critical challenge in adolescence (e.g., Chandler et al., 2003). Therefore, the development of self-event relations is an important way in which adolescents can resolve this challenge. Understanding the development and scaffolding of the capacity for self-event relations in particular, and autobiographical reasoning more broadly, has importance for both a basic understanding of identity development and for understanding how to help adolescents master the challenges of identity continuity. Although self-event relations are not the entire story about autobiographical reasoning or its development, they can illuminate identity processes in both individual and dialogical contexts, can serve as a tool for looking at identity complexity within and across relational contexts, and can serve to connect both narrative approaches to identity and more traditional approaches to self and identity development.

Within this broad frame, several questions strike us as particularly important directions for future work. The first concerns the functional utility of self-event relations for resolving issues of identity continuity, which as we note, has not been tested. Do adolescents who can more effectively draw links between self and experience report a stronger sense of continuity over time directly? Do they show lower rates of risk-oriented behaviors that may indirectly imply continuity problems? A second set of questions concerns the stability of self-event relations over time; given the substantially constructive nature of memory narration, and the emerging perspectives afforded by adulthood and distance, we might expect changes in self-event relations across the transition to adulthood. A third set of questions concerns the implications of the divergent self-event relations that adolescents may construct in different relational contexts. Are these differences problematic? Or are these differences connected to the sophistication and complexity of adolescents' self-views? Some differentiation of self-event relations across different audiences may reflect adaptive flexibility and complexity. However, extremes of differentiation may be akin to fragmentation. What we have offered here, in short, is a toolkit for addressing bigger questions about autobiographical reasoning, identity continuity, and adolescent development.

References

Bluck, S., & Gluck, J. (2004). Making things better and learning a lesson: Experiencing wisdom across the lifespan. *Journal of Personality, 72,* 543–572.

Chandler, M. J., Lalonde, C. E., Sokol, B. W., & Hallett, D. (2003). *Personal persistence, identity development, and suicide.* Oxford, England: Blackwell.

Cleveland, E., & Reese, E. (2005). Maternal structure and autonomy support in conversations about the past: Contributions to children's autobiographical memory. *Developmental Psychology, 41,* 376–388.

Erikson, E. H., & Erikson, J. M. (1997). *The life cycle completed: Extended version.* New York: W. W. Norton.

Fivush, R., & Nelson, K. (2004). Culture and language in the emergence of autobiographical memory. *Psychological Science, 15,* 586–590.

Habermas, T., & de Silveira, C. (2008). The development of global coherence in life narratives across adolescence: Temporal, causal and thematic aspects. *Developmental Psychology, 44*, 707–721.

Habermas, T., & Paha, C. (1999). The development of coherence-relations in adolescents' life narratives: A cross-sectional exploratory study. Unpublished manuscript, Free University of Berlin, Germany.

Harter, S. (1998). The development of self-representations. In N. Eisenberg & W. Damon (Eds.), *Handbook of child psychology, 5th edition* (Vol. 3, pp. 553–617). New York: Wiley.

Locke, J. (1996). An essay concerning human understanding. In K. P. Winkler (Ed.), *An essay concerning human understanding: Abridged and edited with an introduction and notes.* Indianapolis, IN: Hackett.

Marcia, J. E. (1966). Development and validation of ego identity status. *Journal of Personality and Social Psychology, 3*, 551–558.

McAdams, D. P. (1996). Personality, modernity, and the storied self: A contemporary framework for studying persons. *Psychological Inquiry, 7*, 295–321.

McAdams, D. P., & Cox, K. S. (in press). Self and identity across the lifespan. In R. Lerner, A. M. Freund, & M. Lamb (Eds.), *Handbook of lifespan development* (Vol. 2). Hoboken, NJ: Wiley.

McLean, K. C., Breen, A., & Fournier, M. A. (in press). Adolescent identity development: Narrative meaning-making and memory telling. *Journal of Research on Adolescence, 20*, 166–187.

McLean, K. C., & Pasupathi, M. (in press). Old, new, borrowed, and blue? The emergence and retention of meaning in autobiographical storytelling. *Journal of Personality*.

McLean, K. C., Pasupathi, M., & Pals, J. L. (2007). Selves creating stories creating selves: A process model of narrative self development. *Personality and Social Psychology Review, 11*, 262–278.

Pasupathi, M., Carstensen, L. L., Levenson, R. W., & Gottman, J. M. (1999). Responsive listening in long-married couples: A psycholinguistic perspective. *Journal of Non-Verbal Behavior, 23*, 173–193.

Pasupathi, M., & Hoyt, T. (2009). The development of narrative identity in late adolescence and emergent adulthood: The continued importance of listeners. *Developmental Psychology, 45*, 558–574.

Pasupathi, M., & Hoyt, T. (2010). Silence and the shaping of memory: How distracted listeners affect speakers' subsequent recall of a computer game experience. *Memory, 18*, 159–169.

Pasupathi, M., & Mansour, E. (2006). Adult age differences in autobiographical narratives: Integrating experiences with the self. *Developmental Psychology, 42*, 798–808.

Pasupathi, M., Mansour, E., & Brubaker, J. (2007). Developing a life story: Constructing relations between self and experience in autobiographical narratives. *Human Development, 50*(2/3), 85–110.

Pasupathi, M., & Wainryb, C. (in press). On telling the whole story: Facts and interpretations in memory narratives from childhood through adolescence. *Developmental Psychology, 46*, 735–746.

Reese, E., Bird, A., & Tripp, G. (2007). Children's self-esteem and moral self: Links to parent-child conversations. *Social Development, 16*(3), 460–478.

Rice, C. I., & Pasupathi, M. (in press). Reflecting on self-relevant experiences: Adult age differences. *Developmental Psychology, 46*, 479–490.

Schectman, M. (2003). Empathic access: The missing ingredient in personal identity. In R. Martin & J. Barresi (Eds.), *Personal identity* (pp. 94–110). Malden, MA: Blackwell.

Swann, W. B., Jr. (2000). Identity negotiation: Where two roads meet. In E. T. Higgins & A. W. Kruglanski (Eds.), *Motivational science: Social and personality* perspectives. *Key readings in social psychology* (pp. 285–305). Philadelphia: Psychology Press.

Weeks, T. L., & Pasupathi, M. (in press). Integrating negative events within the self: Elaboration, listeners, and gaining insight. *Journal of Personality.*

Weeks, T. L., & Pasupathi, M. (in preparation). Integrating novel events within the self: Expressing meaning and making self. Manuscript in preparation.

Weeks, T. L., & Pasupathi, M. (2010). Autonomy, identity, and narrative construction with parents and friends. In K. C. McLean & M. Pasupathi (Eds.), *Narrative development in adolescence: Creating the storied self* (pp. 65–92). New York: Springer.

MONISHA PASUPATHI is an associate professor of psychology at the University of Utah, Salt Lake City.

TRISHA L. WEEKS is a Ph.D. candidate in the Psychology Department at the University of Utah, Salt Lake City.

Fivush, R., Bohanek, J. G., & Zaman, W. (2010). Personal and intergenerational narratives in relation to adolescents' well-being. In T. Habermas (Ed.), The development of autobiographical reasoning in adolescence and beyond. New Directions for Child and Adolescent Development, 131, 45–57.

4

Personal and Intergenerational Narratives in Relation to Adolescents' Well-Being

Robyn Fivush, Jennifer G. Bohanek, Widaad Zaman

Abstract

Narratives of the self are embedded within families in which narrative interaction is a common practice. Especially in adolescence, when issues of identity and emotional regulation become key, narratives provide frameworks for understating self and emotion. The authors' research on family narratives suggests that adolescents' personal narratives are at least partly shaped by intergenerational narratives about their parents' childhoods. Both personal and intergenerational narratives emerge frequently in typical family dinner conversations, and these narratives reflect gendered ways of being in the world. Adolescents who tell intergenerational narratives that are rich in intergenerational connections and perspective-taking show higher levels of well-being. These findings suggest that individual narrative selves are created within families and across generations. © Wiley Periodicals, Inc.

This research was supported by a grant from the Alfred P. Sloan Foundation to the Emory Center for Myth and Ritual in American Life. We would like to thank Kelly Marin, Mary Ukuku, Davina Mazaroli, Andrea Barrocas, Hanah Gizer, Kelly McWilliams, Amber Lazarus, and Marshall Duke for their contributions to the design of the larger parent project as well as assistance in data collection and coding.

NEW DIRECTIONS FOR CHILD AND ADOLESCENT DEVELOPMENT, no. 131, Spring 2011 © Wiley Periodicals, Inc.
Published online in Wiley Online Library (wileyonlinelibrary.com). • DOI: 10.1002/cd.288

utobiographical narratives are both the process and the product of self-understanding and emotional regulation. We create meaning through creating narratives (Bruner, 1987). The ways in which we recall the events of our lives help to define who we are in the world, and how we understand ourselves and others (Bluck & Alea, 2002; Bluck & Habermas, 2000; Pillemer, 1998). One critical function of autobiographical memory is to use past experiences in ways that allow us to cope with aversive experiences, resolve negative affect, and draw on past emotions in the service of understanding the present and future (Bluck & Alea, 2002; Marin, Bohanek, & Fivush, 2008; Sales & Fivush, 2005; Sales, Fivush, & Peterson, 2003; Pillemer, 1998). Indeed, a great deal of research with adults has demonstrated that adults who are able to narrate the emotional events of their lives in more self-reflective ways show better physical and psychological health (Frattaroli, 2006; Pennebaker & Chung, 2007), indicating that autobiographical narratives play a critical role in regulating emotion.

Autobiographical Narratives Are Socially Constructed

Autobiographical narratives are not individual constructions; narratives of our personal experiences emerge in everyday interactions in which we share the events of our lives with others. Everyday conversation is replete with stories of the past. Whether chatting over the dinner table, talking over the phone, sharing daily activities or favorite stories with friends or family, we share the stories of our lives, and in this process, we reinterpret and reevaluate what these experiences mean to us and for us. Thus, narrative meaning is created in social interactions in which our personal experiences are interpreted and evaluated through social frames and interactions (Conway, Singer, & Tagini, 2004; Fivush, 2008). Moreover, in the give-and-take of daily interaction, we do not simply talk about ourselves; we hear the stories of others. Thus, how we come to understand our personal experiences through socially shared narratives evolves in a context in which we also listen to the stories of others, and these stories can provide powerful frames for the way in which we understand our own experiences (Fivush, Bohanek, & Duke, 2008; Norris, Kuiack, & Pratt, 2004; Mar, Peskin, & Fong, Chapter Six; Pratt & Fiese, 2004).

The Socio-Cultural Perspective. The idea that narrative meaning-making is constructed in social interactions stems from a Vygotskian perspective (1978), in which individual development is conceptualized as occurring within social and cultural contexts that privilege certain skills and knowledge; the social world is organized in ways that highlight certain activities and practices, and children are encouraged to participate in these activities in ways that lead to the development of culturally important skills. Telling and sharing one's personal past is a culturally mediated activity that is more or less valued by particular cultures, and particular members within a culture (Wang & Ross, 2007). In Western culture, having and telling one's autobiography is highly valued (Fivush & Nelson, 2004; McAdams, 2001; Nelson, 2006). From the moment of birth, children are surrounded by stories, stories they tell about themselves, stories others tell about them, and the stories of others (Miller, 1994). Even in the first year of life, well before infants can participate in these narrative interactions, they are hearing about the triumphs and failures of past family members as filtered through the family stories told over and over to entertain, to soothe, and to teach (Fiese, Hooker, Kotary, Schwagler, & Rimmer, 1995; Norris et al., 2004; Thorne, McLean, & Dasbach, 2004). Thus, individual lives are situated within family histories and individual stories are modulated by the stories of others, especially family stories.

Adolescence as a Critical Developmental Period. Narrative meaning-making may become increasingly important in adolescence, as children transition into an adult identity. Several key skills develop and coalesce during adolescence that allow the individual to create more meaningful and more emotionally regulated autobiographical narratives (see Habermas & Bluck, 2000, for a review). First, adolescents become cognitively able to engage in sophisticated perspective-taking, which allows them to understand and integrate the perspective of others into their own views, as well as to integrate their own perspective through time, from past to present and projected into the future (Habermas & Paha, 2001; Harter, 1999). Related to this, adolescents become capable of analyzing and integrating conflicting emotions, and better able to cognitively reframe events in ways that allow for emotional regulation (Compas, Campbell, Robinson, & Rodriguez, 2009; Harter, 1999). Emotional regulation skills may be especially important as adolescents experience increasingly intense and fluctuating emotions (Arnett, 1999), and the parent–child relationship becomes more emotionally labile (Laursen, Coy, & Collins, 1998).

Although we know that personal narratives are important in the developing self-concept and emotional well-being throughout childhood (see Fivush, Haden, & Reese, 2006, for a review), the social and cognitive skills that develop in adolescence allow for a new way of understanding both one's own and others' experiences, through the increasing ability to take the perspective of others and integrate multiple viewpoints, as well as to create a more overarching life narrative that integrates multiple individual experiences (Habermas & de Silveira, 2008; Reese, Yan, Jack, & Hayne, 2009). Thus examining how adolescents create meaning through narratives of self and of others is a window into how adolescents are understanding their experiences in larger social and familial contexts, and how they are using these experiences to understand themselves and their emotions.

The Family Narratives Project

In The Family Narratives Project, my students and I are studying family narrative interactions in multiple contexts in families with pre-adolescents (eight- to twelve-year-olds) and adolescents (fourteen- to sixteen-year-olds), in relation to multiple measures of identity and well-being. We have been particularly interested in personal narratives and intergenerational narratives, specifically the stories adolescents might know about their parents' childhoods. We assess narratives in multiple contexts to gain a broad perspective both on how narratives are created in shared conversations, as family members each contribute and weave a story together, as well as in contexts in which adolescents are asked to independently narrate specific types of events to an interviewer. Following from the sociocultural perspective, we view family co-constructed narratives as a critical context in which parents help adolescents to structure their experiences in ways that allow for emotional expression and regulation, and these skills will be internalized such that family narrative styles will be reflected in the adolescent's own narratives over time. Here, we report on an initial cross-sectional study with adolescents and their families, but based on longitudinal research with younger children, we assume that longitudinal patterns with adolescents will mirror earlier findings that parental reminiscing style influences children's developing narrative skills (see Fivush et al., 2006, for a review).

Narratives Around the Dinner Table. In an initial study, we chose to examine how personal and family narratives emerge in daily social interactions within families with a child transitioning into adolescence, and how these narrative interactions might be related to children's emotional well-being. We focused on family dinnertime conversations, as this is a time when the family comes back together at the end of the day and shares the days' events with each other (see Bohanek, Fivush, Zaman, Lepore, Merchant, & Duke, 2009, for more detail). We assumed we would hear many "Today I..." narratives, stories of what each family member did that day (Blum-Kulka, 1997), and we further assumed that families that shared their daily activities together in more elaborated ways, through collaborative narrative interaction in which family members request, provide, and negotiate information, would facilitate emotional regulation through shared meaning-making. We were curious about the extent to which families would also refer to more remote events, events from the family's past, during a typical dinnertime conversation, and how these stories might be related to children's emotional regulation. We reasoned that if children are constructing meaning for themselves both from their personal experiences and through the experiences of others, then we should see relations to emotional regulation for both personal stories and family stories.

Method. We asked thirty-seven broadly middle-class, ethnically diverse, two-parent families with at least one child between the ages of nine and twelve years old to tape record at least one dinnertime conversation. All members of the family were present during these recordings and the number of children in the family ranged from one to six, with a mean of 2.7. Audio tapes were transcribed verbatim, and two coders jointly examined each transcript and identified narratives that emerged within the dinnertime conversations. A narrative was defined as any mention of a past event, whether earlier that day, last month, or an event from the distant past, such as a story the parent tells about her own childhood. For purposes of these analyses, other topics of conversation over the dinner table, such as talk about future events, talk about general dispositions and traits (e.g., "I know you like pork, that's why I made this."), and talk about general world knowledge (e.g., discussions of how electricity works), were not considered.

Narrative Interaction. Perhaps not surprisingly, narratives accounted for a large proportion of typical family dinner conversations. On average, in a twenty- to thirty-minute dinner, a narrative emerged every five minutes; we identified 235 narratives, with a mean number of 6.35 narratives per family. Most narratives were about recent events, events of that day or the day before (a mean of 4.02 narratives per family), but about a third of all narratives were about remote family events, events that occurred at least several weeks in the past, with the majority of events occurring many years ago (a mean of 2.08 remote narratives per family). Although our initial interest had focused on shared stories, perhaps we should not have been surprised that many families told stories of events that happened to the parents when they were children (26 narratives in all, accounting for 12 percent of all narratives told), which we labeled intergenerational narratives.

Overall, mothers and children contributed more to the narratives (a mean of 161.21 words for mothers and a mean of 139.53 words for children) than did fathers (a mean of 89.54 words). However, although there were more narratives about recent than remote events, once a narrative was initiated, family members contributed as much information about remote as about recent events. That families were so engaged in co-narrating remote family stories suggests that these narratives are an important part of daily family interaction. Indeed, children initiated stories about the family and intergenerational past just as often as did parents, and the high level of involvement in co-narrating these stories suggests that these are narratives that are told frequently and greatly enjoyed.

Family Narratives and Adolescent Well-Being. Provocatively, when we examined relations between participation in family stories across the dinner table and children's emotional well-being, as assessed by the Child Behavior Checklist (CBCL; Achenbach, 1991), which measures both internalizing behaviors, such as anxiety and depression, and externalizing behaviors such as aggression and acting out, we found differential patterns for type of narrative and gender of parent. Mothers who were more involved in co-narrating remote family stories had children who displayed fewer internalizing behaviors. More specifically, mothers who provided more information ($r = -.31$), confirmed more information ($r = -.34$), and negated more information ($r = -.33$), indicating that they were more involved in telling the family story and negotiating what happened, had children with lower internalizing behaviors. In contrast, fathers who were more involved in the "Today I…" narratives, narratives that family members shared about their individual day's activities, had children who displayed fewer behavior problems. Specifically, fathers who solicited their children's "Today I…" narratives through requesting information had children with fewer internalizing ($r = -.32$) and externalizing ($r = -.31$) behaviors. These patterns suggest that parents may play different roles in family narratives, with mothers being the kin-keepers, keeping the family history alive and meaningful (Rosenthal, 1985), and mothers who do this have children with higher levels of emotional adjustment. Fathers, in contrast, tend to spend more time away from the family during the day (even those mothers who worked full time in our sample reported spending more time at home with children than did the fathers). Those fathers who are more involved in catching up on the day's activities and creating new stories for the family have children with higher levels of emotional adjustment.

Intergenerational Narratives. While we were expecting "Today I…" narratives over a typical family dinner, we were somewhat surprised at the number and variability of remote family stories told in this context. That these kinds of family stories, including intergenerational narratives about parents and grandparents, emerge reasonably frequently in daily interaction, and that these stories (at least as co-narrated by mothers) are related to child well-being, suggests that these kinds of narratives provide a framework for adolescents to understand the world and themselves. Some research has suggested that adolescents who incorporate their parent's "voice" into their own narratives, especially about experiences that teach values and morals, show higher levels of well-being (Arnold, Pratt, & Hicks, 2004; Thorne et al., 2004). These studies examine the extent to which adolescents tell a story about themselves that includes lessons provided by their parents, but do not really address the stories that adolescents may know about their parents. Our results suggest that adolescents who are embedded in a storied family history show higher levels of emotional well-being, perhaps because these stories provide larger narrative frameworks for understanding self and the world, and because these stories help provide a sense of continuity across generations in ways that promote a secure identity (see Fivush, Bohanek, & Duke, 2008, for a full theoretical discussion).

Gender Differences in Parent Childhood Stories. Some research has also examined the stories that parents tell their children about their own childhood. These studies have focused on gender differences. Gender identity theory posits that females are more relationship and emotion oriented than are males, whereas males are more achievement oriented (Gilligan, 1982), and research finds that adult females tell autobiographical narratives that are more relationally and emotionally focused than are the autobiographical narratives of adult males (Bauer, Stennes, & Haight, 2003; Fivush & Buckner, 2003; Thorne & McLean, 2002). In line with these findings, mothers tell stories to their preschool children that are more relationship and affiliation oriented and fathers tell stories that are more achievement oriented (Fiese & Bickham, 2004; Fiese & Skillman, 2000). But to date, no one has examined what children take from these stories. What stories might adolescents know about their parents' childhoods and how might these parental intergenerational narratives be related to the adolescents' own well-being?

Method. To explore this idea, we asked 65 fourteen- to sixteen-year-old adolescents from broadly middle-class, racially diverse families to tell us stories they might know about their mothers' and their fathers' childhoods (Zaman & Fivush, 2009). Almost all the adolescents were able to provide two stories they knew about both their mother and their father when they were a child. No adolescent was unable to tell any intergenerational narrative. The narratives varied, from stories about family relationships in the parents' family of origin, interactions with peers, academic achievements, and accidents and mishaps.

We examined these narratives along three dimensions: structure, theme, and content. Structure referred to overall length and level of elaborative detail included on a scale from zero (no elaborative detail) to three (highly elaborative and detailed). Theme was derived from previous research on the stories that parents tell their children described above, and focused on affiliation (scored from 0 for narratives that included no mention of other people to three for narratives that focused explicitly on relationships) and achievement (again with zero for narratives with no mention of achievement and three for narratives that focused on working towards and achieving a specific goal). Finally, content referred to internal state language and included cognitive states (e.g., "My mother *knew* it was wrong."), general affect (e.g., "That was *hard* on her."), and specific emotion words (e.g., "My dad was *happy* about that."). Internal state content has been conceptualized as an integral part of narrative meaning-making, in that it expresses evaluation and interpretation of the experience (Fivush & Baker-Ward, 2005). Further, as already mentioned, there is evidence that females include more internal state language, and especially more emotion, in their autobiographical narratives than do males.

Narratives Told About Mothers and Fathers. Intriguingly, we found few adolescent gender differences in parental intergenerational stories, but both girls and boys told very different kinds of maternal intergenerational narratives than paternal intergenerational narratives. Maternal intergenerational narratives were more elaborative (a mean of 1.61 for mothers and 1.25 for fathers), more affiliative (a mean of 1.44 for mothers and 0.99 for fathers), and contained more general affect (a mean of 1.03 for mothers and 0.66 for fathers) and specific emotion (a mean of 1.02 for mothers and 0.64 for fathers) than paternal intergenerational narratives, suggesting that adolescents are telling these stories as they have been told to them. This further suggests that parental intergenerational narratives may provide adolescents with one way of understanding gender and gendered roles. That adolescent males and females tell stories about their parents' childhoods that differ by parental gender suggests that adolescents are understanding and propagating the gendered roles their parents are narratively portraying.

Narratives Told About Self. What might these gendered messages mean for adolescents' understanding of self and well-being? In addition to narratives of their parents' childhoods, we also asked these same adolescents to tell us narratives about their own personal experiences. Here, we saw the expected pattern of gender differences, with girls telling more elaborated (a mean of 1.84 for girls and 1.33 for boys) and more emotional (a mean of 6.18 for girls and 3.20 for boys) narratives than boys. Interestingly, there were no gender differences in themes of affiliation or achievement in the adolescents' personal narratives. Still, this pattern suggests that adolescents are telling their own stories through their own gendered lens, and they are telling their parents' stories through the gendered lens of the parent.

Relations Between Intergenerational and Personal Narratives. When we examine relations between the personal and intergenerational narratives, girls are telling personal narratives that look very much like their maternal intergenerational narratives; there are significant correlations on almost every narrative variable between these two narratives. However, there are no relations between girls' personal narratives and their paternal intergenerational narratives. For boys, there are no relations between their personal narratives and either their maternal or paternal intergenerational narratives. The patterns suggest that girls are mirroring their mothers' narratives in constructing their own gendered narratives, but it is not clear why boys are not mirroring their fathers (see Peterson & Roberts, 2003 for similar data).

Creating Intergenerational Connections. In collecting these intergenerational narratives, a noteworthy finding emerged. Many of the adolescents drew a specific intergenerational connection between their parents and themselves. These connections included mentioning a specific parallel across generations (e.g., "My dad played soccer when he was young, and that got me started in soccer" or "My mother used to fight with her brother all the time just like I fight with my brother."), reference to life lessons or values (e.g., "She told me about when she used to smoke so that I wouldn't smoke.") or a reference to the current parent–child relationship (e.g., "and now my mom and I read together every night" or "My dad still plays basketball with me every weekend."). These types of intergenerational connections are similar to what Habermas and de Silveira (2008) have described as "autobiographical reasoning" within personal narratives, where adolescents create continuity between multiple individual personal narratives, and to what McLean and Pratt (2006) have termed "life lessons" within personal narratives. The difference is that here, adolescents are drawing these connections between themselves and their parents' experiences, not their own previous experiences.

There were no differences by either gender of adolescent or gender of parent in the occurrence of these connections, but the fact that many adolescents spontaneously made these connections in their intergenerational narratives seemed important, and we thought it might be related to whether adolescents were using these narratives in the service of understanding themselves.

Perspective-Taking in Intergenerational Narratives. In addition, many of the adolescents told intergenerational narratives rich in internal state language, providing information about how their parent thought and felt about the event. This kind of language suggests that the adolescent is taking the perspective of the parent in the narrative, and thus using the parent's experiences as a way of understanding how events in the world unfold and their consequences, possibly as a way of understanding one's own experiences. Thus, we examined relations between the intergenerational connections that adolescents drew in their narratives, their use of internal state language in these narratives and adolescents' emotional well-being, again measured through the CBCL. In this sample, we asked the mother to report on her child's behaviors and we also asked the adolescents to self-report, using the Youth Self-Report, the age-normed self-report form of the CBCL (YSR; Achenbach & Rescorla, 2001).

Intergenerational Narratives and Well-Being. Correlations were computed between the internal state language and intergenerational connections in the narratives and both maternal and child reports of well-being (Zaman & Fivush, 2009). The overall pattern of results indicated that adolescent males who told maternal intergenerational narratives that included more perspective-taking and intergenerational connections self-reported lower levels of externalizing behaviors (rs range from $-.23$ to $-.52$) and, to a lesser extent, lower levels of internalizing behaviors (rs range from $-.21$ to $-.39$). There were similar but fewer relations to paternal intergenerational narratives (rs for internalizing behaviors range from $-.22$ to $-.28$, and externalizing behavior correlated with intergenerational connections at $r = -.37$). For girls, their self-report of well-being was unrelated to either maternal or paternal intergenerational narratives. A different picture emerges using maternal reports of adolescent well-being. Here, girls who included more intergenerational connections and perspective-taking in their narratives about their mothers' childhoods showed lower levels of maternally reported internalizing (rs range from $-.21$ to $-.39$) and externalizing (rs range from $-.37$ to $-.50$) behaviors, but there were no relations to paternal intergenerational narratives, nor were there any relations between maternal reports of adolescent well-being and boys' intergenerational narratives.

Linking Personal and Intergenerational Narratives. Although interpretations of these patterns are complicated, two things are clear. First, for female adolescents, there is both a closer link between their personal narratives and their maternal intergenerational narratives as well as between their maternal intergenerational narratives and their mothers' reports of their well-being. Thus, it seems that when female adolescents take the perspective of their mothers, and use maternal intergenerational narratives to structure their own personal experiences, their mothers report higher levels of adolescent well-being. Second, male adolescents are neither mirroring their parental intergenerational narratives in their own personal narratives nor is their maternally reported well-being related to their parental intergenerational narratives. However, boys who show a higher level of perspective-taking in their maternal and paternal intergenerational narratives self-report higher well-being.

Constructing Gender and Identity Through Narratives of the Familial Past

Clearly, future research will need to elucidate these patterns. Most important, these initial studies were cross-sectional, and longitudinal research is critical in elucidating developmental patterns. Still, these first forays into research on intergenerational narratives and adolescent well-being are provocative. Family narratives, stories about both the family day and the family past, are frequent in everyday interactions, and families that are more engaged in sharing these stories have adolescents who show higher levels of emotional well-being. That adolescents are engaged in co-narrating family stories in everyday interactions suggests that these stories are interesting and important to them. Indeed, adolescents listen to and learn these stories and are easily able to tell stories about their parental intergenerational past.

Moreover, family narrative interaction is a gendered activity. Mothers are more engaged in family stories than are fathers, and mothers that contribute more to keeping the family past alive through such stories have children who show higher levels of emotional well-being. Further, as would be predicted by Vygotskian theory, children are learning the forms and function of family stories through participating in daily family interactions. Family stories tell about gendered lives and provide a framework for understanding the self. Both adolescent males and females tell maternal intergenerational narratives that are more elaborative, affiliative and emotional, and less achievement oriented, than paternal intergenerational narratives, suggesting at least one way in which gender is constructed through narratives and across generations. Further, adolescent girls, at least, seem to be learning how to tell their own gendered narratives through these interactions. Adolescent girls are telling narratives similar in structure and content to their maternal intergenerational narratives, and girls who tell maternal intergenerational narratives higher in intergenerational connections and perspective-taking have higher levels of maternally reported well-being. Although the picture for males is more complicated and awaits further research, the patterns thus far indicate that adolescents are learning how to understand themselves at least partly through family stories. Who we are as individuals emerges in social interactions studded with stories, stories about ourselves and our families in the past that shape who we are in the present and in the future.

References

Achenbach, T. M. (1991). *Manual for the cross-informant program for the CBCL/4-18, YSR and TRF.* Burlington, VT: University Associates in Psychiatry.

Achenbach, T. M., & Rescorla, L. A. (2001). *Manual for the ASEBA School-age forms and profiles.* Burlington, VT: University of Vermont, Research Center for Children, Youth, & Families.

Arnett, J. (1999). Adolescent storm and stress reconsidered. *American Psychologist, 54,* 317–326.

Arnold, M. L., Pratt, M. W., & Hicks, C. (2004). Adolescents' representations of parents' voices in family stories: Value lessons, personal adjustment, and identity development. In M. W. Pratt & B. H. Fiese (Eds.), *Family stories and the life course: Across time and generations* (pp.163–186). Mahwah, NJ: Erlbaum.

Bauer, P. J., Stennes, L., & Haight, J. C. (2003). Representation of the inner self in autobiography: Women's and men's use of internal states language in personal narratives. *Memory, 11,* 27–42.

Bluck, S., & Alea, N. (2002). Exploring the functions of autobiographical memory: Why do I remember the autumn? In J. D. Webster & B. K. Haight (Eds.), *Critical advances in reminiscence work: From theory to application* (pp. 61–75). New York: Springer.

Bluck, S., & Habermas, T. (2000). The life story schema. *Motivation and Emotion, 24,* 121–147.

Blum-Kulka, S. (1997). *Dinner talk: Cultural patterns of sociability and socialization in family discourse.* Mahwah, NJ: Erlbaum.

Bohanek, J. G., Fivush, R., Zaman, W., Lepore, C. E., Merchant, S., & Duke, M. P. (2009). Narrative interaction in family dinnertime conversations. *Merrill-Palmer Quarterly, 55,* 488–516.

Bruner, J. (1987). Life as narrative. *Social Research, 54,* 11–32.

Compas, B. E., Campbell, L. K., Robinson, K. E., & Rodriguez, E. M. (2009). Coping and memory: Automatic and controlled processes in adaptation to stress. In J. Quas & R. Fivush (Eds.), *Emotion and memory in development: Biological, cognitive, and social considerations* (pp. 121–141). New York: Oxford University Press.

Conway, M. A., Singer, J. A., & Tagini, A. (2004). The self in autobiographical memory: Correspondence and coherence. *Social Cognition, 22,* 491–529.

Fiese, B .H., & Bickham, N. L. (2004). Pin-curling grandpa's hair in the comfy chair: Parents' stories of growing up and potential links to socialization in the preschool years. In M. W. Pratt & B. H. Fiese (Eds.), *Family stories and the life course: Across time and generations* (pp. 259–277). Mahwah, NJ: Erlbaum.

Fiese, B. H., Hooker, K. A., Kotary, L., Schwagler, J., & Rimmer, M. (1995). Family stories in the early stages of parenthood. *Journal of Marriage & the Family, 57,* 763–770.

Fiese, B. H. & Skillman, G. (2000). Gender differences in family stories: Moderating influence of parent gender role and child gender. *Sex Roles, 43,* 267–283.

Fivush, R. (2008). Remembering and reminiscing: How individual lives are constructed in family narratives. *Memory Studies, 1,* 45–54.

Fivush, R., & Baker-Ward, L. (2005). The search for meaning: Developmental perspectives on internal state language in autobiographical memory. *Journal of Cognition & Development, 6*, 455–462.

Fivush, R., Bohanek, J. G., & Duke, M. P. (2008). The self in time: Subjective perspective and intergenerational history. In F. Sani (Ed.), *Continuity and self* (pp. 131–143). New York: Psychology Press.

Fivush, R., & Buckner, J. P. (2003). Creating gender and identity through autobiographical narratives. In R. Fivush & C. A. Haden (Eds.), *Autobiographical memory and the construction of a narrative self: Developmental and cultural perspectives* (pp. 149–167.) Mahwah, NJ: Erlbaum.

Fivush, R., Duke, M., & Bohanek, J. G. (2010, February 23). "Do You Know...?" The power of family history in adolescent identity and well-being. *Journal of Family Life.* Retrieved October 4, 2010 from www.journaloffamilylife.org/doyouknow.

Fivush, R., Haden, C. A., & Reese, E. (2006). Elaborating on elaborations: Maternal reminiscing style and children's socioemotional outcome. *Child Development, 77,* 1568–1588

Fivush, R., & Nelson, K. (2004). Culture and language in the emergence of autobiographical memory. *Psychological Science, 15,* 573–577.

Frattaroli, J. (2006). Experimental disclosure and its moderators: A meta-analysis. *Psychological Bulletin, 132,* 823–865.

Gilligan, C. (1982). *In a different voice: Psychological theory and women's development.* Cambridge, MA: Harvard University Press.

Habermas, T., & Bluck, S. (2000). Getting a life: The emergence of the life story in adolescence. *Psychological Bulletin, 126,* 748–769.

Habermas, T., & de Silveira, C. (2008). The development of global coherence in life narratives across adolescence: Temporal, causal and thematic aspects. *Developmental Psychology, 44,* 707–721.

Habermas, T., & Paha, C. (2001). The development of coherence in adolescent's life narratives. *Narrative Inquiry, 11,* 35–54.

Harter, S. (1999). *The construction of the self: A developmental perspective.* New York: Guilford Press.

Laursen, B., Coy, K. C., & Collins, W. A. (1998). Reconsidering changes in parent-child conflict across adolescence: A meta-analysis. *Child Development, 69,* 817–832.

Mar, R. A., Peskin, J., & Fong, K. (2010). Literary arts and the development of the life story. In T. Habermas (Ed.), The development of autobiographical reasoning in adolescence and beyond. *New Directions for Child and Adolescent Development, 131,* 73–84.

Marin, K. A., Bohanek, J. G., & Fivush, R. (2008). Positive effects of talking about the negative: Family narratives of negative experiences and preadolescents' perceived competence. *Journal of Research on Adolescence, 18,* 573–593.

McAdams, D. P. (2001). The psychology of life stories. *Review of General Psychology, 5,* 100–122.

McLean, K. C., & Pratt, M. W. (2006). Life's little (and big) lessons: Identity statuses and meaning-making in the turning point narratives of emerging adults. *Developmental Psychology, 42,* 714–722.

Miller, P. J. (1994). Narrative practices: Their role in socialization and self-construction. In U. Neisser & R. Fivush (Eds.), *The remembering self: Construction and accuracy in the self-narrative* (pp. 158–179). New York: Cambridge University Press.

Nelson, K. (2006). Development of Representation in Childhood. In E. Bialystok & F.I.M. Craik (Eds.), *Lifespan cognition: Mechanisms of change* (pp. 178–192). New York: Oxford University Press.

Norris, J. E., Kuiack, S., & Pratt, M. W. (2004). "As long as they go back down the driveway at the end of the day": Stories of the satisfactions and challenges on grandparenthood. In M. W. Pratt & B. H. Fiese (Eds.), *Family stories and the life course: Across time and generations* (pp. 353–373). Mahwah, NJ: Erlbaum.

Pennebaker, J. W., & Chung, C. K. (2007). Expressive writing, emotional upheavals, and health. In H. S. Friedman & R. C. Silver (Eds.), *Foundations of health psychology* (pp. 263–284). New York: Oxford University Press.

Peterson, C., & Roberts, C. (2003). Like mother, like daughter: Similarities in narrative style. *Developmental Psychology, 39,* 551–562.

Pillemer, D. (1998). *Momentous events, vivid memories.* Cambridge, MA: Harvard University Press.

Pratt, M. W., & Fiese, B. H. (2004). *Family stories and the life course: Across time and generations.* Mahwah, NJ: Erlbaum.

Reese, E., Yan, C., Jack, F., & Hayne, H. (2009). Emerging identities: Narrative and self from early childhood to early adolescence. In K. McLean & M. Pasupathi (Eds.), *Narrative development in adolescence: Creating the storied self* (pp. 23–44). New York: Springer.

Rosenthal, C. J. (1985). Kinkeeping in the familial division of labor. *Journal of Marriage and the Family, 47,* 965–974.

Sales, J. M., & Fivush, R. (2005). Social and emotional functions of mother-child reminiscing about stressful events. *Social Cognition, 23,* 70–90.

Sales, J. M., Fivush, R., & Peterson, C. (2003). Parental reminiscing about positive and negative events. *Journal of Cognition and Development, 4,* 185–209.

Thorne, A., & McLean, K. C. (2002). Gendered reminiscence practices and self-definition in late adolescence. *Sex Roles, 46,* 267–277.

Thorne, A., McLean, K., & Dasbach, A. (2004). When parents' stories go to pot: Telling personal transgressions to teenage kids. In M. W. Pratt & B. H. Fiese (Eds), *Family stories and the life course* (pp. 187–209). Mahwah, NJ: Erlbaum.

Vygotsky, L. S. (1978). *Mind in society: The development of higher psychological processes.* Cambridge, MA: Harvard University Press.

Wang, Q., & Ross, M. (2007). Culture and memory. In S. Kitayama & D. Cohen (Eds.), *Handbook of cultural psychology* (pp. 645–667). New York: Guilford Press.

Zaman, W., & Fivush, R. (2009, April). Intergenerational narratives and adolescent's well-being. Paper presented at the biennial meeting of the Society for Research in Child Development, Denver, CO.

ROBYN FIVUSH *is the Samuel Candler Dobbs Professor of Psychology at Emory University in Atlanta.*

JENNIFER G. BOHANEK *is a postdoctoral research fellow at the Center for Developmental Science at the University of North Carolina at Chapel Hill.*

WIDAAD ZAMAN *is a graduate student in the Department of Psychology at Emory University in Atlanta.*

McKeough, A., & Malcolm, J. (2010). Stories of family, stories of self. In T. Habermas (Ed.), The development of autobiographical reasoning in adolescence and beyond. *New Directions for Child and Adolescent Development, 131,* 59–71.

5

Stories of Family, Stories of Self: Developmental Pathways to Interpretive Thought During Adolescence

Anne McKeough, Jennifer Malcolm

Abstract

Research has shown that a hallmark of adolescent development is the growing capacity to interpret human intentionality. In this chapter, the authors examine developmental change in this capacity, which they have termed interpretive thought, in two types of stories, family and autobiographical, told by Canadian youth aged ten to seventeen years. Illustrative examples reveal that youth coordinate an increasing number of psychological components and in so doing, create increasingly abstract and coherent psychological profiles of self and others. © Wiley Periodicals, Inc.

We wish to thank Kathy Hubley-Caruthers and Deborah Misfeldt Bell for their analysis of the family stories and Diane Salter for her earlier analysis of a corpus of family stories. We also gratefully acknowledge the financial support of the Social Sciences and Humanities Research Council of Canada and the participation of our research volunteers.

Meaning-Making Through Stories

Individuals and cultures constantly strive to make sense of the physical and social world. Whereas the paradigmatic mode of thought organizes the world into categories and concepts and is suited to scientific domains (Bruner, 1986, 1990), the narrative mode of thought is vital to social-psychological meaning making (Bruner, 1986, 1990; Gergen & Gergen, 1988; McAdams, 1993). Stories tell of events that occur over time and social contexts. They also describe people's actions and the intentional states that motivate their actions and specify the causes and consequences of both (Bruner, 1991). Events and people are rendered as culturally familiar in stories when presented as either normative or breaches of the canonical (Bruner, 1991). These features of stories are integrated into a mental framework or schema that is used for perceiving and interpreting the social world. Thus, stories are one way that cultures attribute meaning to experience. By providing cultural models of human action and intention, stories help us order the events of our lives into meaningful experiences (Bruner, 1986, 1990). In a similar way, they help define our purpose, connect with others, and form the basic structures of our identities (McAdams, 1993; Nelson & Fivush, 2004). Thus, not only do stories offer models that help us understand others' intentions and motivations, they also help us understand our own actions, desires, and wishes, as we construct culturally shaped stories that render the events in our lives meaningful.

Autobiographical Memory and Reasoning in the Life Story

The autobiographical stories we construct have the same features as stories in general; however, their content is focused on events and experiences that happen to the self, which are drawn from our autobiographical memory. Autobiographical memories are not eidetic representations of past events, but are rather actively reassembled in ways that help us make sense of personal events (Bluck, Alea, Habermas, & Rubin, 2005). This process of personal construction works together with cultural influences, such as the story schema, to shape autobiographical stories.

When we integrate our autobiographical stories into a coherent whole, we construct our life story (Habermas & de Silveira, 2008). A life story can be seen as a meta-autobiography in that it is the story of our separate stories (McAdams, 1993). The goal of our life story is to provide order to our past, help explain our present, and anticipate our future in light of the past and present. Our life story structures autobiographical memories by integrating them with our understanding of personal attributes, important relationships, and personal and familial history, such that unity, understanding, and continuity in our life are established (Pillemer, 1998). In essence, our identity is achieved and sustained through the life story that we construct (McAdams, 1993).

NEW DIRECTIONS FOR CHILD AND ADOLESCENT DEVELOPMENT • DOI: 10.1002/cd

How are coherent life stories constructed out of separate autobiographical stories? According to Habermas and Paha (2001), with the emergence of adolescence two previously independent capacities, "remembering the past and understanding persons," are coordinated as a result of a growing perception that "the past is not simply there to be retrieved but requires interpretation" (Habermas & Paha, 2001, p. 36). This capacity to reason autobiographically allows adolescents to begin to work toward achieving a cohesive account of the self by, for example, articulating enduring personal states and making reference to biographical background. Through this process, adolescents begin to place the events of their lives within a historical context that helps to explain current circumstances as well as anticipate a future that arises within this context. A sense of identity is constructed in the process of creating a temporally, thematically, and causally coherent narrative that fits with one's cultural conceptions. Autobiographical reasoning, then, is the self-reflective process of creating interpretive links between life's events, which allows adolescents to interpret and evaluate experiences and, in turn, make meaning of their lives (Habermas & Bluck, 2000; Habermas & de Silveira, 2008).

Narrative Interpretive Thought

In our research program, we have also documented this shift to an interpretive stance in adolescence. Whereas Habermas and colleagues (Habermas & de Silveira, 2008; Habermas, & Paha, 2001; Habermas, Ehlert-Lerche, & de Silveira, 2009) have termed the cognitive process *autobiographical reasoning*, given the life story focus of their research, we have termed the process *interpretive narrative thought* (following Bruner, 1986), given the broader focus of our research, which comprises a range of domains, including fictional story composition and comprehension (Genereux & McKeough, 2007; McKeough, 1992; McKeough & Genereux, 2003), family stories, social reasoning and social decision making (McKeough & Griffith, 2010), and life stories (Sanderson & McKeough, 2005) of Canadian youth. More specifically, by applying Case's neo-Piagetian theory to the domain of fictional composition (Case, 1985), we have (a) mapped out the foundational structures of intentional thought that are in place by late childhood, (b) identified a qualitative shift to interpretive thought in early adolescence, and (c) described the increasing complexity of interpretive thought throughout adolescence.

The foundational structures that undergird adolescent interpretive thought reach back to the story schema that young children assemble with the support of parents and caregivers (Reese, Haden, & Fivush, 1993) and their development of a theory of mind (Pelletier & Astington, 2004). As these two fairly independently constructed schemata are coordinated and used in a means–end fashion, children begin to tell what we have referred to as *intentional* stories. In intentional stories, actions and events that occur in the physical world are coordinated with characters' intentions, desires, thoughts, and feelings that occur in the mental world (McKeough, 1992). Throughout middle childhood, children become increasingly adept at describing and integrating what Bruner (1986) has termed the landscapes of action and consciousness.

Whereas ten-year-olds typically focus on proximal intentions and mental states, twelve-year-olds begin to take the mental states themselves as the objects of reflection, thereby engaging in what we have termed *interpretive thought*. Interpretive thought offers a psychological justification of intentions by making reference to, for example, characters' enduring psychological traits or states or their personal history (McKeough, 1992; McKeough & Genereux, 2003). To illustrate, ten-year-olds typically account for a character failing to join in games in terms of a (a) general trait, such as shyness; (b) mental state, such as being mad at his friends; or (c) social rule, such as "It's not right to play with kids if they're not including some people." They do not, however, typically offer justification. That is, a personal past of shyness is not coordinated with an understanding of people (Habermas & Paha, 2001). In contrast, if twelve-year-olds refer to a character as shy, they typically explain the trait in terms of a personal history of rejection and ridicule, for example. Thus, twelve-year-olds simultaneously consider experiences that occurred at different times or in different situations and then extract a higher-order unit of meaning making, such as an explicated personality trait or an enduring psychological state (Habermas & Paha, 2001; Genereux & McKeough, 2007). In other words, they take a meta-position to the character's intentions or desires by coordinating past and present to create an enduring trait. In Chapter 1 Habermas has argued that when adolescents construct a hierarchical category, such as an enduring trait, they establish coherence and mark continuity in their life stories. Not suprisingly, our research has shown that adolescents mark that same coherence and continuity in the lives of their fictional characters through the same process of interpreting intentions within their cultural context.

Our research has also determined that interpretive thought becomes increasingly complex throughout adolescence. A bifocal structure emerges around fourteen years of age (Case, 1985) with the inclusion of competing traits or intentions that create a socio-psychological dialectic and cause a struggle within the character. To illustrate, a character might be torn between wanting to be a cool person but also wanting to be a responsible person (McKeough & Genereux, 2005). This bifocal orientation is one manifestation of adolescents' attempts to explain discontinuities by coordinating two competing desires or intentions that derive from different aspects of their personal history (Habermas & Paha, 2001). By seventeen to eighteen years, as adolescents procede through the elaborated bifocal substage (Case, 1985), this dialectic serves as an integrating device wherein the character transforms as a result of his or her struggles

(McKeough & Genereux, 2003) and gains insight into who and why the self is. For example, an individual who has a life-long commitment to helping others reach their potential might be created through a personal struggle.

Toward a Developmental Model of Adolescents' Personal Stories

Our research program has more recently expanded from a singular emphasis on fictional stories to include personal stories in the form of family stories and life stories. As with our research into fictional stories, our work with family stories and life stories sought to understand the developmental transformation from intentional to interpretive thought between ten and twelve years of age and, further, to explore increases in the complexity of interpretive thought throughout adolescence.

Interpreting Family Stories. Family stories are stories that are told frequently within families about family members, relate some significant event, often represent a family's beliefs and values, and tell of the connectedness and uniqueness of the family. They can also be told simply for entertainment (Stone, 1989). Although family stories share many structural and functional elements with fictional stories, they differ in important ways. First, family stories are not original but have been structured and organized for the listener, usually by an older family member. Therefore, it was important in our research to look beyond the story itself, which is a biographical memory, by having our research volunteers interpret what the story meant to them, that is, to engage in autobiographical reasoning. Second, unlike fictional stories that can be drawn from a range of sub-genres from science fiction to mystery, family stories are personal and serve functions similar to autobiographical memories (Pillemer, 1992). They are sometimes told to help elucidate solutions to problems or give insight into psychological traits or states, and sometimes are told to enhance feelings of closeness through joint reminiscing. The following excerpt about holidays with the extended family clearly illustrates the multiple functions family stories can serve. It was told to and interpreted by Salter (1992) by a seventeen-year-old girl, whom we will call Zoey.

> Zoey: I remember that every year since I was born we would...head out to my grandparent's farm...and everyone would be waiting on the front porch to greet us once more. They would be the best summers that anyone could ask for. The baseball games, running in the fields...There were also those warm summer nights when the house was so packed with parents that all us kids would go outside and sit on the huge front lawn and talk about the good old days, or that day, or what pleasures tomorrow will bring us. (B)ut after fifteen years some of us could not make it down in the summer because of jobs and such. We started to slowly disintegrate one by

one, but the wonderful memories of fifteen wonderful summers will always be there.

Researcher: What's the most important idea in this story?

Zoey: Just relationships,... and the importance of memories. The memories will never fail you... (even when) bad things... are happening.

Researcher: What does the story mean to you?

Zoey: A lot! The story and the memories of it are...really important to me...The whole story's about memories, right? And it's just important to everybody to have memories...and to have a story like that ...

The meaning Zoey's story held for her went far beyond the important experiences of spending summers at the farm and the closeness she felt toward her extended family, although those were certainly important elements. A further meaning was expressed as an abstract concept (i.e., "the importance of memories") that was generalized to other aspects of her life and to the lives of others as well. The dialectics (e.g., joy and sadness; togetherness and family dissolution) in Zoey's story, and her interpretation of them, link past (childhood), present (adolescence), and future (the happy memories to help in darker times) and function to transform her understanding of life. Her response reflects adolescents' capacity to analyze a story's message, apply it to life, abstract truths that also apply to others' lives, and ultimately generalize what might be (Applebee, 1978). In a similar vein, it also reflects what has been termed *gaining insight,* that is "gleaning meaning from an event that applies to greater areas of life than a specific behavior" resulting in "some kind of transformation in one's understanding of oneself or one's relationships with others in general" (McLean & Thorne, 2003, p. 636).

The complexity of Zoey's interpretive thought stands in contrast to that evident in the following prototypic twelve-year-old's interpretation of her family story, which is, nevertheless, insightful in its own right.

Jodi: My story is about when my mom met my dad... (M)y mom thought he was such a dork! He came over to their house all the time and my mom just gradually fell in love with him, and then he popped the question. And now nineteen years later they have great jobs, two wonderful children and my mom still thinks he's a dork!

Researcher: Do you think your mom was trying to teach you something or trying to give you a message?

Jodi: Yes because she was saying "If you meet someone and you don't like them at first, wait because they might grow on you."

Researcher: Has hearing the story ever influenced the way you have acted or thought?

Jodi: Yes. It's influenced me to always give people a chance.

Researcher: Has there ever been a time when thinking about the story helped you in some way?

Jodi: Yes, when this girl was different but I got to know her, and now we are friends.

Although Jodi's interpretation of her family story lacks the abstract quality of Zoey's discussion of the important role of memories in our lives, it clearly has the quality of interpretive thought in that there is a strong psychological focus. Jodi interprets her mother's message and, in so doing, reflects her psychological stance toward others (i.e., "She was saying 'If you don't like someone at first, wait…they might grow on you.'"), generalizes and applies the social teaching to her own life (i.e., "This girl was different…now we're friends."), and references herself psychologically (e.g., "It's influenced me to always give people a chance."). Such responses required Jodi to take a meta-position to proximal mental states, to see across time and social situations, and to extract a higher-order psychological category—taking the time to give someone a chance to show who they are. This type of interpretive thought is also akin to McLean and Thorne's *lessons learned,* that is "learning a specific lesson from an event that could direct future behavior in similar situations" (McLean & Thorn, 2003, p. 636).

The following ten-year-old's family story interpretation differs markedly from the two preceding samples.

Alec: One day my mom told me that when my brother was little he always used to put his foot down the toilet. One day my brother put his foot down the toilet (and it got) stuck. So my dad had to unscrew the toilet and take him outside. So he tried to pull on his leg. So we had to break open the bottom of the toilet. Just then his foot came out. And his foot was fine.

Researcher: What is the most important idea in the story?

Alec: To unscrew the toilet and take it outside.

Researcher: Do you think your mom was trying to teach you something or trying to give you a message?

Alec: Yes. Do not stick your foot down the toilet.

Researcher: Has there ever been a time when thinking about the story helped you in some way, maybe to understand something or to figure something out?

Alec: No. I don't stick my foot down the toilet.

Alec's construal of his family story is markedly literal. Although he is able to extract a social rule of sorts from the story (i.e., "Do not stick your

NEW DIRECTIONS FOR CHILD AND ADOLESCENT DEVELOPMENT • DOI: 10.1002/cd

foot down the toilet.") and coordinate it with a reference to his own action (i.e., "I don't stick my foot down the toilet."), he fails to reflect on his brother's, mother's, or his own mental states, or on the rule.

From this analysis, we concluded that on average, by twelve years of age, young adolescents had developed the capacity to begin to interpret family stories on a psychological level, and that this capacity continued to develop through the later teen years. Prior to that point, our Canadian research volunteers seemed unable to look to past events to inform their present and future.

Autobiographical Stories. Guided by the work of McAdams (1993) and Habermas and Bluck (2000), we extended our research to typically developing adolescents' key life stories events. Following McAdams (1993) we asked our research volunteers to narrate their life story and highlight three critical events in their lives: a high point, a low point, and a turning point. Our aim was to determine if volunteers' orally produced low, high, and turning point stories would become increasingly interpretive from ages twelve years to eighteen years of age and follow a pattern similar to fictional and family stories.

In sum, not only did our findings support the previous developmental analyses, they also offered new insights into the ways adolescents bring interpretive thought to bear on events in the process of meaning-making. That is, we observed elaborated interpretive thought in the stories of the oldest group, where abstract principles informed understanding of personal events, competing personal traits were integrated, and life events were situated in a context that extended the personal past through to the present and on into the future. The following sample turning point story, told by Karen, exemplifies this type of thought.

Karen: Well on Saturday morning…my Dad made a cutting remark to my Mom…and my Dad and I are screaming at each other, and he said something like, "Well, now you're not going to have to worry about it any more!" And I said, "What's that supposed to mean?" He said, "We're splitting up." So it wasn't a surprise to me but at the same time it—my heart was being ripped out of my chest…I mean, I have always worried about it…but them telling me—the first thing that occurred to me was that nothing would ever be the same…I don't know why it bothered me so much because at the same time it was so relieving, but I knew that nothing was ever going to be the same…I know it was kind of self-serving but at that point I was thinking: "What about me? Where am I going to go from here?"…And now it's like that road is—is collapsed and I've got to carve out a whole new path for myself.…It was difficult…I was never one of those people who liked change…I'd rather stay static than to go through the uncomfortableness…

Researcher: What difference has it made in your life?

NEW DIRECTIONS FOR CHILD AND ADOLESCENT DEVELOPMENT • DOI: 10.1002/cd

> Karen: It's—it's taught me to be a lot more self-dependent …It's made me grow up in the sense that this was a really challenging road to go down and I certainly learned and grew and changed more than in any other period in my life. I really learned to be self-motivating and self-preserving.

In this excerpt, Karen analyzes her character by describing a series of psychological dialectics in her past, such as being extremely bothered yet relieved and not being surprised yet feeling extremely upset, and her present, such as preferring the status quo yet carving out a new path. Moreover, she uses the tension created between the conflicting elements to transform herself into a new person who has become increasingly "self-motivating and self-preserving" as she has learned and grown to be less "self-serving." This transformative self-referencing, which allowed her to anticipate a safe future, is the hallmark of elaborated bifocal interpretive in the seventeen-year-olds' autobiographical stories and is reminiscent of McLean and Thorne's (2003) gaining insight. Further, as the preceding and subsequent sample stories demonstrate, although we see similar structural components in both family and autobiographical stories, the psychological content of the two differ substantially in that the two types of narratives are inherently different in the degree of personal significance they hold for the individual.

The interpretive thought of fourteen-year-olds included social and psychological dialectics that took the form of conflicting social rules and psychological traits (bifocal interpretive), but the dialectics did not serve a transformative function, as Sam's low-point story illustrates.

> Sam: I was down in the States for summer vacation and my dad got a call…saying that (my friend) had passed away. So we drove [home]…and, I don't know, it was a pretty sad car ride. No one talked or anything like that…And I had a talk at the funeral…It just kind of knocked me down a few pegs and made me realize that…life really can really kind of fade pretty quick. I think maybe I was in shock a bit because you just never expect someone your own age to die…At first I was in disbelief until I finally saw him. Then I was just so sad…It kind of made me more cautious about what I do. That life is not something you can take for granted, so you have to be careful. But it kind of made me realize that…I should kind of pretty much live the most each day.

In interpreting this low point event, Sam presents contrasting insights into life, "You have to be careful" and "live the most of each day," but fails to integrate them in a way that brings new meaning to his life. Similar to Karen's interpretation story, Sam evokes a cultural axiom that the experience has made him stronger, but unlike Karen, he has not provided sufficient elaboration to conclude that he has gained enhanced self-understanding.

NEW DIRECTIONS FOR CHILD AND ADOLESCENT DEVELOPMENT • DOI: 10.1002/cd

Although twelve-year-old volunteers' stories evidenced interpretive thought, it was typically less complex than that of the seventeen- and fourteen-year-olds. Their responses, nevertheless, demonstrated they were clearly able to interpret events from a psychological perspective and generalize to identify a trait or psychological state. Most twelve-year-olds did not, however, discuss alternatives or elaborate on why they changed psychologically. The following story excerpt, told by Dianna, illustrated this level of interpretive thought.

Dianna: Ok, in grade four, I guess, me and (Erin), we had this big fight and...it was about something really stupid...We got really pissed off at each other and we just said really mean things to each other. And we just left and didn't speak to each other for a couple of months. At the time I was really sad that we had broken up...and that we weren't hanging around with each other and stuff. And I was kind of lonesome. And, yeah, a couple of months later, (Marya) started hanging around with both of us, and we started hanging around together again, just because we were hanging around with her. And we just became friends again, and we've been friends ever since.

Researcher: What made that a turning point for you?

Dianna: Well I think it just matured the relationships I had with my friends... [Erin] has been a really good friend for me, especially since then.

Researcher: Has that changed you in any way?

Dianna:...I realized...it's stupid to fight over something so small and then not talk to someone for a long time.

In this story, Dianna reflects on the event psychologically, realizing the futility of her anger. Although she states that she and her relationships with friends have changed, there was, however, little explanation to describe how the relationship had matured. Furthermore, she failed to move to the next interpretative level by asserting that friendship, in general, is more important than inconsequential arguments and, thus, her abstract generalizations are less evident. Dianna's interpretation shows little evidence of insightful application beyond her immediate situation, but does demonstrate that she has learned a lesson from her experience (McLean & Thorne, 2003).

Summary

These analyses allow us a glimpse into the transformations that interpretive narrative thought undergoes throughout adolescence, supporting the widely held position that narrative thought constitutes our main mode of social meaning making (Bruner, 1990). Case's (1985) developmental theory offers a way to move beyond these generalities, however, by offering a framework with which to map out the specific nature and development of adolescents' interpretive narrative thought. Case has proposed that maturational-based increases in processing capacity allow and, at the same time, set a ceiling on developmental growth, which results in a predictable progression toward increasingly complex thought structures throughout each major stage (Case, 1985). More specifically, during adolescence, neurological maturation of the frontal lobes enhances the development of executive functions, which permits higher order thinking (Case, 1992) such as interpretive narratives (McKeough & Griffith, 2010). As well, domain-specific experience is necessary for developmental growth, as it provides the culturally shaped frameworks to which executive processes apply (Case, 1985, 1992). In short, the complementarities of neurological maturation and experience afford adolescents the capacity to construct increasingly complex narratives where the "engine of action" resides in the psychology of the character rather than in the sequence of events that make up the plot (Bruner, 1986, p. 37).

It is this de-emphasis of plot and emphasis on the character's psychology that we see in adolescents' autobiographical reasoning; their focus is more on interpreting events rather than merely recounting them. This allows them to present a more integrated and cohesive account of the event, themselves, and their belief system, as well as to develop a more comprehensive theory of personal meaning-making. Thus, as they develop, adolescents increasingly engage in self-reflection and create integrated storied accounts that situate events in their lives in a historical past, which allows them to understand the present and anticipate the future. In so doing, they create accounts of self that are temporally, thematically, and causally coherent, which support their development of a narrative identity.

References

Applebee, A. (1978). *The child's concept of story: Ages two to seventeen.* Chicago: The University of Chicago Press.

Bluck, S., Alea, N., Habermas, T., & Rubin, D. C. (2005). A tale of three functions: The self-reported uses of autobiographical memory. *Social Cognition, 23,* 91–117.

Bruner, J. (1986). *Actual minds, possible worlds.* Cambridge, MA: Harvard University Press.

Bruner, J. (1990). *Acts of meaning.* Cambridge, MA: Harvard University Press.

Bruner, J. (1991). The narrative construction of reality. *Critical Inquiry, 18,* 1–21.

Case, R. (1985). *Intellectual development: Birth to adulthood.* Toronto: Academic Press.

Case, R. (1992). The role of the frontal lobes in the regulation of cognitive development. *Brain and Cognition, 20*(1), 51–73.

Genereux, R., & McKeough, A. (2007). Transformation in narrative thought during adolescence: The structure and content of narrative interpretation. *British Journal of Educational Psychology, 77*(3), 1–25.

Gergen, K. J., & Gergen, M. M. (1988). Narrative and the self as relationship. *Experimental Social Psychology, 21*, 17–76.

Habermas, T. (2010). Autobiographical reasoning: Arguing and narrating from a biographical perspective. In T. Habermas (Ed.), The development of autobiographical reasoning in adolescence and beyond. *New Directions for Child and Adolescent Development, 131*, 1–17.

Habermas, T., & Bluck, S. (2000). Getting a life: The emergence of the life story in adolescence. *Psychological Bulletin, 126*, 748–769.

Habermas, T., & de Silveira, C. (2008). The development of global coherence in life narratives across adolescence: Temporal, causal and thematic aspects. *Developmental Psychology, 44*, 707–721.

Habermas, T., Ehlert-Lerche, S., & de Silveira, C. (2009). The development of the temporal macrostructure of life narratives across adolescence: Beginnings, linear narrative form, and endings. *Journal of Personality, 77*, 527–560.

Habermas, T., & Paha, C. (2001). The development of coherence in adolescents' life narratives. *Narrative Inquiry, 11*, 35–54.

McAdams, D. P. (1993). *The stories we live by: Personal myths and the making of the self.* New York: William Morrow & Co.

McKeough, A. (1992). The structural foundations of children's narrative and its development. In R. Case (Ed.), *The mind's staircase: Stages in the development of human intelligence* (pp. 171–188). Hillsdale, NJ: Erlbaum.

McKeough, A., & Genereux, R. (2003). Transformation in narrative thought during adolescence: The structure and content of story compositions. *Journal of Educational Psychology, 95*(3), 537–552.

McKeough, A., & Griffith, S. (2010). Adolescent narrative thought: Developmental and neurological evidence in support of a central narrative structure. In M. F (Ed.) *The development of relations among mind, brain, and education* (pp. 213–229). New York: Springer Verlag.

McLean, K., & Thorne, A. (2003). Late adolescents' self-defining memories about relationships. *Developmental Psychology, 39*(4), 635–645.

Nelson, K., & Fivush, R. (2004). The emergence of autobiographical memory: A social cultural developmental theory. *Psychological Review, 111*, 486–511.

Pelletier, J., & Astington, J. W. (2004). Action, consciousness and theory of mind: Children's ability to coordinate story characters' actions and thoughts. *Early Education and Development, 15*(1), 5–22.

Pillemer, D. (1998). *Momentous events, vivid memories.* Cambridge, MA: Harvard University Press.

Reese, E., Haden, C. A., & Fivush, R. (1993). Mother-child conversations about the past: Relationships of style and memory over time. *Cognitive Development, 8*, 403–430.

Salter, D. (1992). A cognitive developmental analysis of the interpretation of family stories by adolescents and pre-adolescents. Unpublished Masters thesis, University of Calgary, Alberta, Canada.

Sanderson, A., & McKeough, A. (2005). A narrative analysis of behaviorally troubled adolescents' life stories. *Narrative Inquiry, 15*(1), 127–160.

Stone, E. (1989). *Black sheep and kissing cousins.* New York: Harper and Row.

ANNE MCKEOUGH *is a professor in applied psychology at the University of Calgary, Alberta, Canada.*

JENNIFER MALCOLM *is a sessional instructor at Mt. Royal University, Calgary, Alberta, Canada.*

NEW DIRECTIONS FOR CHILD AND ADOLESCENT DEVELOPMENT • DOI: 10.1002/cd

Mar, R. A., Peskin, J., & Fong, K. (2010). Literary arts and the development of the life story. In T. Habermas (Ed.), The development of autobiographical reasoning in adolescence and beyond. *New Directions for Child and Adolescent Development, 131*, 73–84.

6

Literary Arts and the Development of the Life Story

Raymond A. Mar, Joan Peskin, Katrina Fong

Abstract

Throughout adolescence, children begin to develop their life story: a coherent account of their experiences and selfhood. Although the nature of this development is still being uncovered, one promising direction for research is the examination of factors that could encourage life story development. Here the authors explore the idea that exposure to the literary arts (i.e., poetry and fictional literature) might promote the formation of a coherent autobiographical narrative. Taking a critical look at both theoretical proposals along with the current empirical research, they provide a brief survey of this intriguing hypothesis. © Wiley Periodicals, Inc.

NEW DIRECTIONS FOR CHILD AND ADOLESCENT DEVELOPMENT, no. 131, Spring 2011 © Wiley Periodicals, Inc.
Published online in Wiley Online Library (wileyonlinelibrary.com). • DOI: 10.1002/cd.290

When we reflect back upon our life, we can interpret our experiences as being organized around an underlying theme, such as "loneliness," "social injustice," or "the meaning in the order of the universe," and this allows us to interpret scattered events as consistent and integrated (Csikszentmihalyi & Beattie, 1979). This process of autobiographical reasoning (Habermas, Chapter One) allows for emotional personal memories to contribute to overarching frameworks that structure the self, memory, and identity. Forming a life story, these frameworks integrate experience from the past with our effort to understand the present along with goals for the future (Bluck & Habermas, 2000; Habermas & Bluck, 2000). Not surprisingly, our life story has important implications for how we see ourselves and who we see ourselves as (McLean, Pasupathi, & Pals, 2007). It is therefore important to consider how this life story develops.

The central quality of life stories is their coherence, or how tightly the elements of the story can be seen to form a whole (Habermas & Bluck, 2000; McAdams, 2006; cf. Nicolopoulou, 2008). Life stories have a narrative structure, separate from other forms of discourse (Berman & Nir-Sagiv, 2007), and interestingly the ability to employ a narrative form appears to develop earlier than expository discourse (Berman & Katzenberger, 2004). There is a clear developmental trajectory from the ages of around four to twelve, with children becoming increasingly more skilled in producing fictional stories that possess a strong narrative structure (Reid, 1999; Ukrainetz et al., 2005). However, it is not until adolescence that children begin to exhibit a capacity for creating their own autobiographical story, integrating several events distant in time into a coherent thematic whole, and this occurs well after the emergence of expository discourse. Throughout adolescence the coherence of these life stories increases, with children increasingly able to produce more integrated representations of their personal history (Habermas & Paha, 2001; Habermas & de Silveira, 2008). Because the ability to create a coherent narrative for a specific life episode buffers this memory from distortion (Kulkofsky & Kiemfuss, 2008), an interesting possibility arises: The ability to create a coherent life story might result in a more stable self-identity. In light of this possibility, it is important to consider what might promote or foster the development of a coherent life story. According to theorists such as McLean (2008), the life story schema—a rudimentary knowledge framework for how a life progresses—develops from self-reflection, both thinking and talking about one's past. One interesting possibility is that exposure to the literary arts, such as poetry and fictional literature, might provide a novel context for such thinking, and thus support the development of coherent life stories by helping to organize personal experience (Mackenzie, 1989). In this chapter, we take a critical look at the ideas and evidence behind this possibility.

NEW DIRECTIONS FOR CHILD AND ADOLESCENT DEVELOPMENT • DOI: 10.1002/cd

Fiction and Autobiography: Theoretical Links

There are a number of complex interactions between our personal experience and the experience of reading. The mind's representation of knowledge in literary reading can be seen in terms of dynamic cognitive frameworks, such as the life story, that the reader brings to the text, but these frameworks are in turn also shaped by the reading (Dias & Hayhoe, 1988). Bluck and Habermas (2000) emphasize the importance of an extended lifetime perspective that enables individuals to look back over their lives and conceptualize an enduring value or motivation to explain their life trajectory. However, many adolescents have not reached the point at which they can look back over their lives; reading literature might help to provide this much broader perspective of the life span. It has been noted, for example, that biographies and autobiographies are directed toward readers eleven or twelve years of age at the youngest, approximately the same time that we see other evidence of an emerging life story (Habermas & Bluck, 2000).

Children as young as the age of four begin to recognize the structural elements of narratives (Lynch et al., 2008), and as they enter into their early teens they begin to derive multiple levels of meaning from these literary narratives (Genereux & McKeough, 2007). When interpreting the behavior of characters, adolescents also increasingly begin to make attributions for behavior based on enduring personality traits (Genereux & McKeough, 2007), perhaps indicating an increasing awareness of an integrated "whole person" as actor. This developmental trend toward the recognition of personality traits and personal history is also evident in the fictional stories that adolescents create (McKeough & Genereux, 2003). Might exposure to literary narratives increase the likelihood of forming a personal life narrative that integrates personal history to create a similarly holistic representation?

Building on McLean's proposal (2008) regarding the importance of self-reflection for developing coherent life stories, literary narratives do seem to spur autobiographical thinking. In a recent study, adolescents made interpretations of a short story that centered on the death of a young woman's husband. One participant, a high school student, stated, "As much as I feel for her, as the saying goes '___' happens [sic]. Everyone loses people. You have to overcome adversity if you want to succeed. I wanted to be a pilot, but because of some archaic rule, I can't, I deal. I lost my grandmother tragically, but while I do not forget her, I continue my life" (Wells Jopling, 2008, p. 68).

In interpreting this short story, this adolescent is clearly involved in self-reflective autobiographical thinking, integrating her own history and viewing it in light of the themes and events of the story. She seems not only to be rehearsing and developing the integration of aspects of herself, but she is also using it in her textual interpretation, that is, "integrating the present moment with the life already lived" (Bluck & Habermas, 2000, p.141).

A form of literary theory known as *reader response theory* theorizes that "the reader's existing stock of experience acts as a referential background against which the unfamiliar can be conceived and processed" (Iser, 1994, p. 144). The derivation of meaning while reading involves an interaction between three basic components: (1) the vantage point represented in the text, (2) the reader's own perspective, and (3) the place where these sets of perspectives converge (Iser, 1994). In this way, the textual interpretation itself becomes a part of the ongoing development of the reader's self-identity. Another way in which autobiography interacts with the reading of literary fiction is when readers draw on personal life experiences to help create the world presented by the author (Rosenblatt, 1989).

The above examples show how individuals' life themes can provide an evaluative filter by means of which new information is encoded and made meaningful (Bluck & Habermas, 2000; Csikszentmihalyi & Beattie, 1979). In his book on teaching literature in school, Sumara (2002) points out the importance of the remembered experience of the reader. He argues that reading activities, in which students interpret both personal and collective experience, "illuminate the processes by which humans experience a sense of personal identity, and how these experiences are necessarily organized by remembered identifications and relationships" (Sumara, 2002, p. 24).

Reading fiction might allow adolescents to reason about the whole lives of characters, giving them specific insight into an entire lifespan without having to have fully lived most of their own lives. An important aspect of life stories is incorporating personal discontinuities, resolving these seeming inconsistencies, and creating a coherent representation of one's life. In fiction, characters often evolve and change, yet remain the same person, providing meaningful exemplars for how people can undergo a variety of experiences, act very differently in different situations, grow and change in a number of ways, and yet maintain their individual personhood. Authors also often provide details of a character's past as a way to explain his or her current personality and future behaviors. Doing so might encourage readers to look back at their own experiences and consider how these fit into their overall life schema.

Fiction and Autobiography: Research Evidence

An important question is whether empirical evidence exists to support the idea that reading literature encourages students to develop, rehearse, or use their life story schema. Despite the intriguing theoretical reasons to believe that this may be the case, this topic has remained largely unexplored. As a result, little research directly examines this question. Consequently, we review what indirect research there exists that relates to this

NEW DIRECTIONS FOR CHILD AND ADOLESCENT DEVELOPMENT • DOI: 10.1002/cd

question, with the caveat that none of these studies provides a direct test of the hypothesis.

In terms of indirect evidence, the findings are not encouraging. One study that approached this topic from quite a unique direction looked at children who either had, or did not have, an imaginary friend (Trionfi & Reese, 2009). Children who had an imaginary friend were better at telling fictional stories than those who did not, and these children were also better at narrating past experiences. Importantly, there were no differences in vocabulary or narrative comprehension ability for the two groups, which means that a better ability to narrate one's past was not correlated with better story comprehension. It is important to note that narrative comprehension ability is not the same as exposure to fictional narratives, so the implications of this study for our central hypothesis are not without question.

Other approaches have not yielded any greater support for the idea that reading fiction helps the development of a life story. In a large-scale study by the National Literacy Trust, 8000 students aged five to seventeen years were asked "why they read" (Clark & Foster, 2005). Of the younger, primary students, 39 percent endorsed the statement, "It helps me understand more about myself," but this dropped to 17 percent among the older, secondary students. This decline might seem surprising; however, a similar finding was reported in another large study (van Schooten & de Glopper, 2003) in which students from the seventh to eleventh grades completed a questionnaire measuring literary response (Miall & Kuiken, 1995). One aspect of this questionnaire measures "insight," characterized by items such as, "When I begin to understand a literary text, it's because I've been able to relate it to my own concerns about life," and "I often see similarities between events in literature and events in my own life." Insight scores were fairly low among this sample, and furthermore, decreased from grades seven to eleven. This apparent trend toward less insight, and less of a tendency to draw relations between the self and the text, runs counter to the theory that reading literary fiction aids the formation of coherent life narrative throughout adolescence. A separate interpretation of this finding, however, is that adolescents increasingly see literature as aesthetic objects, not necessarily tied to their own lives. In which case, life narratives and autobiographies might similarly be treated in an aesthetic manner, as part of a developmental trend, with less of a discouraging implication for the hypothesis in question.

One other way we can examine the possibility that reading fictional literature helps adolescents develop a coherent life narrative is to capitalize upon naturally existing differences in reading habits. Census data from Canada shows that women are more likely to read than men (Statistics Canada, 1998), and this difference emerges at a young age; girls are consistently found to be more interested in voluntary reading than boys (Morrow & Weinstein, 1986). The more important question, from our perspective, may be whether these gender differences persist when looking at individuals who do not engage in *any* pleasure-reading at all. This does appear to be the case. More boys than girls reported spending no time at all reading for pleasure (Nippold, Duthie, & Larsen, 2005), and this appears true across cultures and across generations. A large longitudinal study from Sweden, for example, found that the proportion of non-readers was much higher among boys than girls, regardless of age group (eleven- to twelve-year-olds or fifteen- to sixteen-year-olds), and at every time point tested from 1976 to 2002 (Johnsson-Smaragdi & Jönsson, 2006). Given the fact that boys are more likely to be non-readers than are girls, we would expect there to be parallel gender differences in quality of life narratives if reading aids the development of a coherent life story. In line with this idea, there is some evidence that girls are better at producing fictional stories than boys (McKeough & Genereux, 2003). Does this also translate to the creation of a life narrative?

A survey of the available research does not appear to provide much support for this idea. Awareness of the cultural conventions regarding construction of a biography do not appear to differ between males and females across adolescence (from ages eight through twenty; Habermas, 2007). There are also no gender differences with respect to the quality of narrative structure in life stories across this same time period (Habermas, Ehlert-Lerche, & de Silveira, 2009), or differences for other variables related to content and quality (McAdams et al., 2006). Lastly, there do not appear to be any differences in the capacity for young men and young women to derive meaning from their life stories (e.g., McLean & Breen, 2009). In light of the gender differences observed for reading behavior, this lack of difference for multiple aspects of life narratives is inconsistent with the idea that reading fiction could aid the development of life stories. Again, it is important to stress that this does not constitute a direct test of this possibility.

The available research on whether exposure to literary fiction influences life stories is thus rather discouraging, despite a number of intriguing theoretical reasons to posit such a relation. Admittedly, however, this research is largely indirect and loosely inferential. Perhaps the safest thing to conclude is that a good empirical examination of this hypothesis has yet to be conducted. What indirect work does exist seems consistent, however, with a recent study demonstrating that explicit training fails to produce improvements in the coherence of life stories (Habermas & de Silveira, 2008). It is possible that a more interactive approach to improving life stories is necessary. In line with this proposal, responsive listeners provoke more meaning-laden conversations regarding personal experience (Pasupathi & Hoyt, 2009); an intervention designed along these lines might be promising. We now turn our attention to the theoretical arguments and empirical research regarding the related proposal that reading poetry may help improve the quality of life stories.

Poetry and Autobiography: Theoretical Links

In the interpretation of poetry, individuals often draw on personal experiences. In a recent intervention study involving disguised symbolism (Peskin & Wells-Jopling, 2009), adolescents were presented with poems that could be interpreted either literally or symbolically. For instance, William Carlos Williams' (1998) poem "Poem—As the Cat" could be interpreted literally as a poem about a cat that climbs over the top of the jam cupboard and then "carefully" steps down "into the pit of/the empty/flowerpot." However, many adolescents viewed the cat and empty flowerpot as open-ended symbols, which allowed them to provide their subjective and very personal choice of topic (Gibbs, 1994). For instance, one young girl demonstrated her concern that women need to be wary, "Like the cat in the poem, women are thought to be cautious; however, they may just be stepping into a trap." Others related the poem to their own loneliness, or to how the world obeys its own rules, or to the emptiness of life.

These interpretations can often take the shape of themes. The formation of thematic coherence within life stories "involves individuals' capacity to step back from recalled experiences and extract metaphors, lessons, or messages" (Singer & Bluck, 2001, p. 95), such as "Living is struggling," "People cannot be trusted," "Family is of the utmost importance," or "Overcoming obstacles" (McLean, 2008; Ruth, Birren, & Polkinghorne, 1996). This has obvious import for reading poetry, which often explores similar coherent themes. Reading poetry may help the reader explore themes for his or her own life; these are then used to organize experiences in a coherent way.

The open-ended nature of poetry might encourage the examination, rehearsal, and projection of one's own life story schema during interpretation. Myers (1998) suggests that when poems are carefully selected they have the potential to elicit intense emotional and sensory reactions such that students "may become motivated to seek the written word as a means to explore and understand the complexities of their personal lives" (p. 170). At the first major John Keats research conference, an essay by a high school senior was read to the audience. Written by "Clay," a student who frequently skipped school and drove a truck with a "Born to Party" bumper sticker, it read, "How do I relate to Keats? Hell, I am John Keats. My life struggles are his poetry" (Walton, 1995).

Poetry and Autobiography: Research Evidence

Just as with literary fiction, there has been no direct research on whether the reading of poetry might influence a person's life story despite the compelling theoretical reasons for postulating such a link. Research that informs this question indirectly, however, does exist. One promising piece of indirect evidence can be seen in the distinction between *point-driven reading* in contrast to *story-driven reading* (Beach, 1987). Point-driven reading is when the reader explores and construes the point or significance of the text, determined largely by their individual experience and personality; story-driven reading, in contrast, is when the reader is primarily interested in the plot (Vipond & Hunt, 1984). Although point-driven reading is the most appropriate approach when it comes to reading almost all literary genres (Miall, 1990), it applies particularly well to the reading of poetry. According to Culler (1976), the poetry reader expects that a poem will express "a significant attitude to some problem concerning man[kind] and/or his relation to the universe" (p. 115). English teachers are also more likely to encourage text reading that is point-driven, and this might explain why Swedish adolescents who received more literary instruction and read more literature were better able to provide symbolic meaning when reading poetry (Svensson, 1987). In this study, students with less reading experience provided more literal and story-driven interpretations. Intriguingly, this finding posits a relation between the reading of literary fiction and the reading of poetry, within the context of uncovering meaning and symbolic importance that could in turn have an impact on one's life story.

In later adolescence, students begin to develop an appreciation of the aesthetic elements of literary texts that add a layer of meaning, and this growing aesthetic appreciation might inform their own life narratives as well. In a recent think-aloud study of students (fourth, eighth, and twelfth grades) reading texts in the shape of poems, Peskin (2010) found that the twelfth graders but not the younger students appreciated the aesthetic elements of the texts. The fourth and eighth graders merely elaborated on the content. Those in the fourth grade tended to describe their personal experiences or memories in relation to the content: "It reminds me of World War Two because I saw a man walking up the street during World War Two." The eighth graders related to the content less in terms of their own personal memories than in terms of their own knowledge of the world: "Bad things...are going on in the world today...kids out on the street and homeless people dying from the coldness outside and...there's nothing you can do about it." The twelfth graders, on the other hand, talked about the poems as involving multiple meanings and metaphoric content, and as expressing a significant attitude to some issue related to the human condition. These older students paid attention not only to what the poem was saying, but how the author was saying it; how the sounds, the contrasts, and other textual devices amplified the subject matter. The years between the ninth and twelfth grades appear to be a time when literature is increasingly being conceptualized from an aesthetic point of view. This growing aesthetic viewpoint might help to create more meaningful and coherent life narratives. Notably, this finding concerning poetry supports the alternative explanation for why adolescents increasingly report drawing less insight from literary fiction, that is, they are viewing these texts more and more as aesthetic objects.

Conclusions

There are sound theoretical reasons to believe that exposure to the literary arts might promote development of a coherent life story. Both literary fiction and poetry promote autobiographical thinking, as readers draw relations between their own lives and the content of the text, while extracting overarching themes. Literary fiction also provides a unique opportunity for adolescents to adopt a lifespan perspective, examining how the events in a character's life contribute to shape a holistic identity. Research evidence that directly tests this hypothesis has yet to be conducted, however, and the indirect evidence that exists is not encouraging. Although a gender difference exists with regard to leisure reading, no parallel gender difference is present for various aspects of life story development. As well, readers increasingly view literary texts as less relevant to their own lives as they enter adolescence, and report decreasing interest in drawing personal insight from literature. It is possible, however, that this increasing distance reflects a growing tendency to view literary fiction and poetry as aesthetic objects, objects that may promote the identification of personal life themes.

Although the indirect evidence that exists is not particularly promising, the true question of interest has not been tackled empirically. To do so, a preliminary study would have to be done in which reading habits were measured and life stories recorded, with adolescents being the most likely population as this appears to be when life stories emerge (Habermas & Bluck, 2000). Coherence and quality of these life stories would be evaluated and quantified, and the correlation between coherence and exposure to poetry and literature assessed. If exposure to the literary arts is correlated with life story coherence and quality, an experimental design would be adopted to determine causality. Specifically, individuals would have to be randomly assigned to read different sorts of texts, with life stories recorded before and after this intervention. If reading literature and poetry does aid the development of better life stories, then we would expect those assigned to read these types of texts to exhibit a greater increase in life story quality compared to those assigned to read other types of texts. Writing literary fiction and writing poetry might also encourage coherence in an adolescent's life narrative and this possibility should be examined as well.

Researching participation in and exposure to the literary arts has already yielded a number of promising insights into human development. Reading is a well-known predictor of early vocabulary acquisition (Sénéchal & LeFevre, 2002), and it appears that exposure to children's storybooks might also influence social development. Parent–child bookreading is correlated with child theory-of-mind abilities (Adrian, Clemente, Villanueva, & Rieffe, 2005), and expertise in choosing children's literature on the part of mothers predicts teacher ratings of child empathy and socio-emotional development (Aram & Aviram, 2009). Parental ability to recognize the authors and titles of children's storybooks from among a list of foils also predicts better theory-of-mind performance in children, even after controlling for the child's vocabulary, age, gender, and parental income (Mar, Tackett, & Moore, 2010). This growing body of evidence that exposure to the literary arts may influence child development in a domain separate from language acquisition seems very promising. Although there is much that is unknown about the development of life stories, how participation with the literary arts influences life stories seems a fruitful area to direct empirical attention.

References

Adrian, J. E., Clemente, R. A., Villanueva, L., & Rieffe, C. (2005). Parent–child picture-book reading, mothers' mental state language and children's theory of mind. *Journal of Child Language, 32,* 673–686.

Aram, D., & Aviram, S. (2009). Mothers' storybook reading and kindergartners' socioemotional and literacy development. *Reading Psychology, 30,* 175–194.

Beach, R. (1987). Differences in autobiographical narratives of English teachers, college freshman, and seventh grade author(s). *College Composition and Communication, 38,* 56–69.

Berman, R. A., & Katzenberger, I. (2004). Form and function in introducing narrative and expository texts: A developmental perspective. *Discourse Processes, 38,* 57–94.

Berman, R. A., & Nir-Sagiv, B. (2007). Comparing narrative and expository text construction across adolescence: A developmental paradox. *Discourse Processes, 43,* 79–120.

Bluck, S., & Habermas, T. (2000). The life story schema. *Motivation and Emotion, 24,* 121–147.

Clark, C., & Foster, A. (2005). *Children's and young people's reading habits and preferences: The who, what, why, where and when.* London, England: National Literacy Trust.

Culler, J. (1976). *Structuralist poetics: Structuralism, linguistics and the study of literature.* Ithaca, NY: Cornell University Press.

Csikszentmihalyi, M., & Beattie, O. V. (1979). Life themes: A theoretical and empirical exploration of their origins and effects. *Journal of Humanistic Psychology, 19,* 46–63.

Dias, P., & Hayhoe, M. (1988). *Developing response to poetry.* Milton Keynes, England: Open University Press.

Genereux, R., & McKeough, A. (2007). Developing narrative interpretation: Structural and content analyses. *British Journal of Educational Psychology, 77,* 849–872.

Gibbs, R. W. (1994). *The poetics of mind: Figurative thought, language and understanding.* New York: Cambridge University Press.

Habermas, T. (2007). How to tell a life: The development of the cultural concept of biography. *Journal of Cognition and Development, 8,* 1–31.

Habermas, T. (2010). Autobiographical reasoning: Arguing and narrating from a biographical perspective. In Habermas, T. (Ed.), The development of autobiographical reasoning in adolescence and beyond. *New Directions for Child and Adolescent Development, 131,* 1–17.

Habermas, T., & Bluck, S. (2000). Getting a life: The emergence of the life story in adolescence. *Psychological Bulletin, 126,* 748–769.

Habermas, T., & de Silveira, C. (2008). The development of global coherence in life narratives across adolescence: Temporal, causal, and thematic aspects. *Developmental Psychology, 44,* 707–721.

Habermas, T., Ehlert-Lerche, S., & de Silveira, C. (2009). The development of the temporal macrostructure of life narratives across adolescence: Beginnings, linear narrative form, and endings. *Journal of Personality, 77*, 527–560.

Habermas, T., & Paha, C. (2001). The development of coherence in adolescent's life narratives. *Narrative Inquiry, 11*, 35–54.

Iser, W. (1994). Readers and the concept of the implied reader. In D. Keesey (Ed.), *Contexts for criticism* (pp. 137–144). London: Mayfield Publishing Company.

Johnsson-Smaragdi, U., & Jönsson, A. (2006). Book reading in leisure time: Long-term changes in young peoples' book reading habits. *Scandinavian Journal of Educational Research, 50*, 519–540.

Kulkofsky, S., & Kiemfuss, J. Z. (2008). What the stories children tell can tell about their memory: Narrative skill and young children's suggestibility. *Developmental Psychology, 44*, 1442–1456.

Lynch, J. S., van den Broek, P., Kremer, K. E., Kendeou, P., White, M. J., & Lorch, E. P. (2008). The development of narrative comprehension and its relation to other early reading skills. *Reading Psychology, 29*, 327–365.

Mackenzie, P. (1989). The contribution of "story" to children's development. *Early Child Development and Care, 46*, 63–75.

Mar, R. A., Tackett, J. L., & Moore, C. (2010). Exposure to media and theory-of-mind development in preschoolers. *Cognitive Development, 25*, 69–78.

McAdams, D. P. (2006). The problem of narrative coherence. *Journal of Constructivist Psychology, 19*, 109–125.

McAdams, D. P., Bauer, J. J., Sakaeda, A. R., Anyidoho, N. A., Machado, M. A., Magrino-Failla, K., White, K. W., et al. (2006). Continuity and change in the life story: A longitudinal study of autobiographical memories in emerging adulthood. *Journal of Personality, 74*, 1371–1400.

McKeough, A., & Genereux, R. (2003). Transformation in narrative thought during adolescence: The structure and content of story compositions. *Journal of Educational Psychology, 95*, 537–552.

McLean, K. C. (2008). Stories of the young and the old: Personal continuity and narrative identity. *Developmental Psychology, 44*, 254–264.

McLean, K. C., & Breen, A. V. (2009). Processes and content of narrative identity development in adolescence: Gender and well-being. *Developmental Psychology, 45*, 702–710.

McLean, K. C., Pasupathi, M., & Pals, J. L. (2007). Selves creating stories creating selves: A process model of self-development. *Personality and Social Psychology Review, 11*, 262–278.

Miall, D. S. (1990). Reader's responses to narrative: Evaluating, relating, anticipating. *Poetics, 19*, 323–339.

Miall, D. S., & Kuiken, D. (1995). Aspects of literary response: A new questionnaire. *Research in the Teaching of English, 29*, 37–58.

Morrow, L. M., & Weinstein, C. S. (1986). Encouraging voluntary reading: The impact of a literature program on children's use of library centers. *Reading Research Quarterly, 21*, 330–346.

Myers, M. P. (1998). Passion for poetry. *Journal of Adolescent and Adult Literacy, 41*(4), 262–271.

Nicolopoulou, A. (2008). The elementary forms of narrative coherence in young children's storytelling. *Narrative Inquiry, 18*, 299–325.

Nippold, M. A., Duthie, J. K., & Larsen, J. (2005). Literacy as a leisure activity: Free-time preferences of older children and young adolescents. *Language, Speech, and Hearing Services in Schools, 36*, 93–102.

Pasupathi, M., & Hoyt, T. (2009). The development of narrative identity in late adolescence and emergent adulthood: The continued importance of listeners. *Developmental Psychology, 45*, 558–574.

Peskin, J. (2010). The development of poetic literacy through the school years. *Discourse Processes, 47,* 77–103.

Peskin, J., & Wells-Jopling, R. (2009, April). *Are difficulties with symbolic thinking a result of cognitive maturational constraints? A developmental intervention study.* Poster presented at the biennial meeting of the Society for Research in Child Development, Denver, CO.

Reid, D.F. (1999). *The acquisition of narrative syntax.* Unpublished doctoral dissertation, University of South Carolina, Columbia.

Rosenblatt, L. M. (1989). The transactional theory of the literary work: Implications for research. In C. R. Cooper (Ed.), *Researching response to literature and the teaching of literature,* (pp. 32–53). New York: Ablex Publishers.

Ruth, J-E., Birren, J. E., & Polkinghorne, D. E. (1996). The projects of life reflected in autobiographies in old age. *Aging and Society, 16,* 677–699.

Sénéchal, M., & LeFevre, J. (2002). Parental involvement in the development of children's reading skill: A five-year longitudinal study. *Child Development, 73,* 445–460.

Singer, J. A., & Bluck, S. (2001). New perspectives on autobiographical memory: The integration of narrative processing and autobiographical reasoning. *Review of General Psychology, 5,* 91–99.

Statistics Canada. (1998). *General social survey.* Ottawa, Ontario, Canada: Author.

Sumara, D. (2002). *Why reading literature in school matters: Imagination, interpretation, insight.* Mahwah, NJ: Erlbaum.

Svensson, C. (1987). The construction of poetic meaning: A developmental study of symbolic and non-symbolic strategies in the interpretation of contemporary poetry. *Poetics, 16,* 471–503.

Trionfi, G., & Reese, E. (2009). A good story: Children with imaginary companions create richer narratives. *Child Development, 80,* 1301–1313.

Ukrainetz, T. A., Justice, J. M., Kaderavek, J. N., Eisenberg, S. L., Gillam, R. B., & Harm, H. M. (2005). The development of expressive elaboration in fictional narratives. *Journal of Speech, Language, and Hearing Research, 48,* 1363–1377.

van Schooten, E., & de Glopper, K. (2003). The development of literary response in secondary education. *Poetics, 31,* 155–187.

Vipond, D., & Hunt, R. A. (1984). Point-driven understanding: Pragmatic and cognitive dimensions of literary reading. *Poetics, 13,* 261–277.

Walton, B. (1995, September). *The art of teaching Keats.* Paper presented at The John Keats Bicentennial Conference, Cambridge, MA.

Wells Jopling, R. (2009). *Awareness of author motivation in adolescents' responses to fictional narrative.* Unpublished doctoral dissertation, University of Toronto, Canada.

Williams, W. C. (1998). *The collected poems of William Carlos Williams: Volume I.* Alexandria, VA: Chadwyck-Healey, Inc.

RAYMOND A. MAR *is an assistant professor of psychology at York University, Toronto, Canada.*

JOAN PESKIN *is associate professor of psychology at the University of Toronto, Canada.*

KATRINA FONG *is a first-year master's student in psychology at York University, Toronto, Canada.*

Mclean, K. C., & Mansfield, C. D. (2010). To reason or not to reason: Is autobiographical reasoning always beneficial? In T. Habermas (Ed.), The development of autobiographical reasoning in adolescence and beyond. New Directions for Child and Adolescent Development, 131, 85–97.

7

To Reason or Not to Reason: Is Autobiographical Reasoning Always Beneficial?

Kate C. McLean, Cade D. Mansfield

Abstract

Autobiographical reasoning has been found to be a critical process in identity development; however, the authors suggest that existing research shows that such reasoning may not always be critical to another important outcome: well-being. The authors describe characteristics of people such as personality and age, contexts such as conversations, and experiences such as transgressions, which may hinder adaptive reasoning. They also propose alternatives to autobiographical reasoning for managing challenging events and constructing the life story, which include different kinds of meaning-making than those primarily focused on in the current literature. © Wiley Periodicals, Inc.

We thank Andrea Breen, Lewis Webster Jones, and Jennifer Pals Lilgendahl for especially thoughtful and encouraging critiques. We also thank Western Washington University for an internal grant to the first author for completion of this manuscript.

NEW DIRECTIONS FOR CHILD AND ADOLESCENT DEVELOPMENT, no. 131, Spring 2011 © Wiley Periodicals, Inc.
Published online in Wiley Online Library (wileyonlinelibrary.com). • DOI: 10.1002/cd.291

Autobiographical reasoning is actively reflecting on one's personal past to make explicit connections between that past and oneself (Habermas & Bluck, 2000). We argue that although autobiographical reasoning is a critical process for identity development related to maturity and well-being (e.g., King, Scollon, Ramsey, & Williams, 2000; McAdams et al., 2004; McLean & Pratt, 2006; Pals, 2006a), there are certain persons for whom, and certain events and contexts in which, reasoning about the past and the self is detrimental to well-being. Although we agree with the authors in this volume and others that reasoning is a critically important narrative process, we suggest that the demands put on us by our audiences, our internal resources, our experiences, and our culture can facilitate as well as limit the benefits of autographical reasoning.

Autobiographical reasoning is a critical part of the process of forming a life story (Habermas & Bluck, 2000), such that to selectively appropriate events into one's life story one must reason about them to integrate them into that larger story (Pasupathi, Mansour, & Brubaker, 2007). We define autobiographical reasoning as explicit reasoning that serves to connect events to the self to create a story of personal continuity (Habermas & Bluck, 2000; Pasupathi et al., 2007)—that is, reasoning is evident in narratives that include self-event connections (Pasupathi et al., 2007), lessons and insights (e.g., McLean & Thorne, 2003), patterns of complexity and growth (Pals, 2006b), and the redemption of past negative events (McAdams, 2006). Of course, these types of reasoning can result in different outcomes. For example, reasoning about stability of the self is less complicated than reasoning about personal change (e.g., McLean, 2008a; Pasupathi et al., 2007). Reasoning about nuances of a past event (e.g., complexity) is different than redeeming it, and these two processes have different implications for well-being (e.g., King et al., 2000).

Research has clearly shown the importance of autobiographical reasoning in relation to well-being (e.g., King et al., 2000; Lilgendahl & McAdams, in press; Mansfield, McLean, & Lilgendahl, in press; Pals, 2006a), identity status development (McLean & Pratt, 2006), explaining oneself to close others (McLean & Pasupathi, in press), and understanding negative life events (Pals, 2006a). However, we argue that the events one is reasoning about, the context of reasoning, and personal characteristics matter for the degree to which reasoning predicts well-being, which we define broadly in discussing relevant studies (but see Pals 2006a; King et al., 2000).

Events: What Should We (Not) Reason About

Past research has clearly shown that all events are not created equal when it comes to autobiographical reasoning. For example, negative, disruptive, and challenging events appear to require more reasoning than do expected and/or positive events (e.g., Bruner, 1990; McLean & Thorne, 2003; Thorne, McLean, & Lawrence, 2004). Indeed, parents begin to scaffold rudimentary forms of autobiographical reasoning at a young age by providing more explanation of negative than positive events (e.g., Bird & Reese, 2006). Thus, reasoning about a brush with cancer may bring some peace, but reasoning about one's wedding day may not. In fact, trying to explain positive events may undermine well-being (Lyubomirsky, Sousa, & Dickerhoof, 2006), perhaps because a wedding day is part of the canonical life story (e.g., Habermas, 2007) and thus does not need to be explained (Bruner, 1990).

Nevertheless, even within traumatic events there are limits to the efficacy of reasoning. Baumeister, Stilwell, and Wotman (1990) have argued that we distance ourselves from events in which we harm others to maintain positive self-perceptions (see also Pasupathi, McLean, & Weeks, 2009; Mansfield, McLean, & Lilgendahl, in press). When harm is directed at the self there are also limits to the efficacy of autobiographical reasoning. Consider a study by Fivush and Sales (2006), in which they examined how mother–child dyads discussed acute (visiting the emergency room for an asthma attack) and chronic (the ongoing conflict of controlling the child's asthma) stressors. Somewhat surprisingly, children of mothers who helped them develop especially detailed narratives of the acute stressor were not likely to cope more effectively than children whose mothers scaffolded a less detailed narrative. In contrast, for narratives of chronic stressors, children whose mothers provided an emotional and explanatory framework for understanding the stressor had the highest well-being. Thus, the event being reasoned about (harming others or the acute versus chronic nature of a difficult experience) and the context of that reasoning, having a good scaffolder in this case, are as important to well-being as how one reasons about the event. We note that although detailed scaffolding is not autobiographical reasoning on the child's part, it has been suggested that this kind of scaffolding sets the stage to develop reasoning processes in adolescence and adulthood (e.g., McLean, Pasupathi, & Pals, 2007).

Contexts: When Should We (Not) Reason

Less work has been done on the contexts that facilitate autobiographical reasoning, but it appears that conversational contexts, in particular, demand different kinds of reasoning. McLean and Pasupathi (in press) found that between newly dating romantic partners reasoning that centers on self-stability is more common and adaptive than reasoning focused on self-change, perhaps by diminishing uncertainty about who we are with close others (e.g., De La Ronde, & Swann, 1998). Similarly, there is also a risk in sharing vulnerable stories, to which some audiences are uncomfortable responding (Thorne & McLean, 2003), as well as risks to elaborative narration that come with distracted listeners (Pasupathi & Hoyt,

2009). These studies suggest that certain kinds of reasoning may be limited by contexts and listeners; hence, studies comparing across contexts and listeners are needed.

Studies that focus on the implications of reasoning in solitude versus reasoning with others are also needed. For example, research has shown that writing about past traumatic events in ways that lead to cognitive understanding and less negative emotion improves health over time (Pennebaker & Seagal, 1999). Further, writing or talking to oneself about past negative events seems to be more advantageous than just thinking about such events (Lyubomirsky et al., 2006). Though these studies have not defined these linguistic markers as autobiographical reasoning, they do suggest that the ability to form a coherent account of the past, perhaps by engaging in autobiographical reasoning, may be a part of the process that leads to well-being. Writing and talking aloud to oneself may facilitate the process of finding coherence; however, talking to real audiences may not. That is, once the talking turns social, the choice of audience may matter for how well one is able to create a coherent story (e.g., Thorne & McLean, 2003). It is clear that some people need scaffolding to make a coherent story; nevertheless, it may also be that once one has some reasoning tools (by adolescence or adulthood), the time and lack of judgment afforded by solitary reasoning is important for creating the kind of story that is associated with good health.

Finally, different cultures vary in views of what constitutes the self (Markus & Kitayama, 1991), and cultures define the content and processes of autobiographical reasoning. For example, Caucasian Americans tend to have more elaborated, self-focused memory narratives than do the Chinese (Wang, 2001), and these are characteristics that are central to the kind of reasoning we are discussing. Wang (2001) suggested that self-focused reasoning reflects the individualism of American culture. It is not that Chinese individuals are not engaging in autobiographical reasoning, but that such reasoning may look different in Chinese culture. Thus, cultural contexts demand different kinds of reasoning, and some may require more or less reasoning of the kind discussed here to achieve well-being.

Persons: Who Should (Not) Reason

Pasupathi and Mansour (2006) suggested that the question of whether autobiographical reasoning is adaptive depends on the person. We delineate personal characteristics that may predict unsuccessful reasoning, specifically age and personality.

Age. It is now clear that autobiographical reasoning is a developmental accomplishment. Habermas and de Silveira (2008) examined autobiographical reasoning in individuals aged eight, twelve, sixteen, and twenty, with half of the participants receiving training in autobiographical reasoning and half receiving no such training. In predicting autobiographical

NEW DIRECTIONS FOR CHILD AND ADOLESCENT DEVELOPMENT • DOI: 10.1002/cd

reasoning, they examined this training, repeated narration, number of negative life events, frequency of biographical practices, age, and intelligence quotient (IQ); only age consistently predicted higher reasoning. This suggests that developmental achievements may have occurred to make reasoning more likely and that, for young children, reasoning about the past may not be possible or beneficial. Indeed, Fivush, Marin, Crawford, Reynolds, and Brewin (2007) found that children (aged nine through thirteen) who were instructed to write about emotions and explanations of problems had lower well-being over time compared to those who wrote about problems without instructions to elaborate on emotions and explanations. This is in marked contrast to research with adults that has shown that such writing improves well-being over time (Pennebaker & Seagal, 1999). Further, in early adolescence autobiographical reasoning in written narratives is associated with lower well-being (McLean, Breen, & Fournier, in press). McLean et al. (in press) provide one explanation for these findings by noting that those who spend more time in deliberative reasoning may have experienced more difficult life events, which could be a third variable that predicts lower well-being in early adolescence. However, this is not necessarily the case in studies with adults. Indeed, Fivush et al. (2007) suggested that those at younger ages need the scaffolding that occurs in conversation to facilitate the emotional regulation skills and reframing of past events necessary for successful reasoning (see also Polkinghorne, 2004). Of course, all of these interpretations should be taken with caution, as the results are correlational.

At the other end of the life span, it appears that older adults reason in less complex ways than younger people. For example, older adults are more likely to reason about stable aspects of the self compared to younger adults (McLean, 2008b; Pasupathi & Mansour, 2006). Further, reasoning about stability is associated with higher well-being for older adults, and reasoning about change is associated with higher well-being for younger adults (McLean, unpublished data). Thus, one may be less likely to accommodate change with age as there is already a consistent theme to one's life that is maintained by reasoning about self-stability (McLean & Fournier, 2008). Another potential explanation for these age differences is socio-emotional selectivity theory (Carstensen, 1991), which suggests that with age, we focus more on emotion and, relative to younger people, older individuals are especially focused on positive affect. Considering temporal scarcity and shortened time horizons for the elderly, their focus on positive affect may be more adaptive than extended autobiographical analysis of the past (cf., Wong & Watt, 1991). Thus, whereas younger children may not be equipped for autobiographical reasoning, older adults may not find it necessary to reason with the same intensity as younger adults (McLean & Lilgendahl, 2008).

Personality. A variety of studies have examined how personality relates to autobiographical reasoning. McLean and Fournier (2008) coded the degree to which individuals reported effortfully engaging in autobiographical reasoning. This effort was associated with the trait of conscientiousness and ego development, suggesting that personality characteristics that may facilitate the engagement with autobiographical reasoning. Further, McAdams and colleagues (McAdams et al., 2004) found that narrative complexity is associated with openness to experience. These studies raise the possibility that those with more curiosity about and attention to novelty and variety in life experiences and who are more complex in their thinking have more complex narratives with greater conceptual differentiation and integration, two important parts of autobiographical reasoning.

Yet, just because those who score higher on conscientiousness, openness to experience, and ego development reason about the past more than those who scored lower on these characteristics does not mean that they are happier because of it (see Bauer, McAdams, & Sakaeda, 2005; Loevinger, 1976, for correlational findings and theoretical considerations). Indeed, there are cases in which low openness predicts lower reasoning, but not lower well-being. This is perhaps best evidenced in analyses of George W. Bush, who is someone who is at the bottom of the barrel on openness, not an analytical reasoner, but seemingly happy (Rubenzer & Faschingbauer, 2004).

At another level of personality, autobiographical reasoning is associated with how wise one is, particularly when reasoning about especially difficult events, such as transgressions (Bluck & Gluck, 2004; Mansfield et al., 2009). Indeed, choosing the appropriate issues to reason about— those that are most meaningful to the self and that one can do something about—are a reflection of wisdom that is relevant to adaptive reasoning (Kennedy-Arlin, 1990; Kitchener & Brenner, 1990). However, those who are wiser are not necessarily happier, as the deeply analytic characteristic of wisdom may be associated with unease or uncertainty for those who think deeply about the self and the world (e.g., Loevinger, 1976).

Where Does Understanding the Limitations of Autobiographical Reasoning Lead Us?

The cultural press for autobiographical reasoning is implicit (or perhaps explicit) in the nature of much of the research discussed in this volume (including our own), as well as in our society. Constructing a personal life story is a critical part of one's identity in individualistic cultures (e.g., McAdams, 1996; Wang & Brockmeier, 2002), which makes autobiographical reasoning a demand of our culture. That is, we expect people to story themselves (e.g., Bruner, 1990; McAdams, 2001), to reason in those stories (Habermas & Bluck, 2000), to redeem trauma (McAdams, 2006), and to think of themselves as consistent across time (McLean & Pasupathi, in press). Yet, what of the people without helpful scaffolders, who are less open to experience or less wise, whose stories are too rife with trauma to redeem—what are these people to do in the face of this cultural press?

Resilience Not Reasoning. We want to make a difficult argument, which is that there are some people for whom, and some contexts in which, autobiographical reasoning may be detrimental. We, as optimistic Americans, want to think that the possibility exists for everyone to develop a redemptive and well-reasoned life story, regardless of their experiences and characteristics. Yet something has nagged at us as we look at our data—some people do not seem to be able to reason, or, if they are, it is not associated with higher well-being. For example, we have data from at-risk youth in which there are individuals who have had particularly challenging lives, but have decided to put themselves on a positive path. Yet this change is shown in behavior and positive statements about the current self without linking that self to the past (Breen, 2010). For example, in our dataset one teen answering questions about her childhood showed marked incoherence, which could have been rectified with autobiographical reasoning.

P: I had a pretty good childhood; I mean, I'd go and see my dad and then sometimes I'd go and hang out with my mom and I had lots of family so it was a pretty good, like everybody else.

I: Okay. Can you think of a specific memory from childhood that comes to mind?

P: Mmm, not really. I mean, when I was little I used to travel a lot...and...with my fa...with my uncle because my dad was in jail so we would travel to go see him so...traveling was the only thing I could really remember about being little.

This participant had difficulty reasoning about, and even remembering, her past. Her example of her "good" childhood was seeing her father in jail, a statement that calls out for reasoning. She was able, however, in the course of the interview to talk coherently about her current self and future goals. She discussed her growing maturity, her desire for a family and to be a teacher—all without linking those things to her past. Perhaps to maintain this positive self-perception she cannot reflect on the past because it would be too challenging to her current view. If redemption is important to well-being, then people with terrifically challenging lives seem somewhat doomed unless they come up with a more positive story. Yet if one has few positive experiences to select for inclusion in one's life story, then the only option might be to develop a narrative that avoids details in favor of broad themes (e.g., I can't remember visiting my dad in jail, but overall my life was really happy). This might be a good strategy for putting oneself on a path to resilience, in which case it is not the lack of reasoning that is not optimal, but the experiences themselves which leave the person no "productive" option for a reasoned narrative (Breen, 2010).

The pattern we have just described may not be limited to those with challenging pasts. Indeed, individuals in normative samples protect self-esteem through their subjective appraisals of the self over time (Ross & Wilson, 2002). That is, regardless of how much time has passed since an event, individuals appraise the self that is capable of negative events as temporally distant from their current self and appraise the self capable of positive events as temporally closer. Thus, Ross and Wilson (2003) suggest that people protect themselves by seeming to be "getting better all the time."

Bonanno and colleagues have examined the management of trauma across varied contexts, such as loss, childhood sexual abuse, and the 9/11 attacks, identifying an individual difference manifested in response to trauma called *repressive coping* (Bonanno, 2005; Bonanno et al., 2007; Coifman, Bonanno, Ray, & Gross, 2007). Repressive copers report little negative affect when discussing their traumas although they simultaneously show heightened physiological response (Coifman et al., 2007), suggesting a disconnect between physiologic arousal associated with the trauma and their self-reported state. Although we have to interpret the consequences of this apparent disconnect with caution, it may be that genuinely failing to experience strong negative emotion when discussing the trauma may weaken the need to reason about it. Indeed, if these individuals are experiencing negative emotion and not admitting it, that repression of emotion (and the repression of reasoning to explain that emotion) appears to be beneficial. Several studies have shown that repressive copers are less likely to experience depression, anxiety, and posttraumatic stress disorder, and have less somatic complaints at as far as 18 months posttrauma (Coifman et al., 2007).

Westphal and Bonanno (2007) suggest that resilience in the face of trauma may arise from personal characteristics, such as optimism and hardiness, which preclude the need for posttraumatic growth (see also Pressman & Bonanno, 2007). Though these findings stand in contrast to the notion that posttraumatic growth is related to autobiographical reasoning (e.g., McLean & Pratt, 2006; Pals & McAdams, 2004), these studies and others (e.g., Ross & Wilson, 2003) suggest that for some individuals it may be most psychologically adaptive to spend less time reasoning about their most troubling past events and relegating them to a past self while hardily moving on.

Alternatives to Autobiographical Reasoning. Once research begins to cohere, as the literature on autobiographical reasoning is doing, it will be useful to step back to see if we are missing other relevant parts of the story. Whereas one part of the story has to do with individual differences, contexts, and experiences that might preclude reasoning, another part of the story has to do with examining other kinds of reasoning. In focusing on explicit and linguistic modes of reasoning, we may be missing other processes that communicate the thread of one's life story that we as researchers have not examined in depth (see also Fivush & Baker-Ward, 2005).

In thinking about characteristics of stories that will delineate explicit autobiographical reasoning, some researchers have discussed small and big stories (e.g., Bamberg, 2004; McLean & Thorne, 2006; Pasupathi, 2006; Thorne, 2004). Big stories are those that are part of the life story—turning points, self-defining memories, and so forth. These big stories are where we look for, and often find, autobiographical reasoning. Small stories are those that are told in conversation, but may not be a part of one's larger life story, and thus may not include extensive reasoning. Yet, these small stories may go far in communicating one's identity (Bamberg, 2004), as reasoning may not only be in the representation of the story, but in the performance of it. If you tell a funny story, it means that you are funny, and you do not need to state explicitly that you are a funny person for the audience.

From another perspective, reasoning may not be necessary because some meanings are culturally understood parts of a life story. This may explain why one does not need to reason about one's wedding day—that is expected to be a wonderful love story. Building on this idea, Fivush (in press) has described narrators being voiced or silenced, and traditionally, silence was viewed as a marker of less power—one does not disclose or detail one's story for fear of misunderstanding or rejection. Recently, however, Fivush (in press) has argued that silence can also signal the acknowledgment of shared understandings that are likely to be culturally dominant (see also Weststrate & McLean, 2010). Thus, reasoning may not be necessary because some stories come with shared meaning that we may be missing in looking for explicitly stated reasoning.

Conclusion

We first note that many of the studies we have discussed are correlational in nature and, thus, we do not know if reasoning causes well-being, well-being causes reasoning, if there is a reciprocal relationship between the two, or if there is a third variable causing the association. Thus, we make our statements about the causal role of reasoning for well-being with caution, but we note some of the experimental (Lyubomirsky et al., 2006; Pennebaker & Seagel, 1999) and theoretical work (e.g., McLean et al., 2007; Pals, 2006a; King, 2001) that points to at least a partial role of reasoning for well-being.

Indeed, the now robust field of autobiographical reasoning has shown us that it is a critical process that enhances and deepens the life stories that our culture values. Yet as we step back from this rich set of studies, we see that there are caveats that we may want to spend some more time examining and illuminating. Our argument rests on the idea that the degree to which autobiographical reasoning is beneficial to one's well-being will depend on the interaction between characteristics of the person and the contexts of reasoning. We also note that we have defined benefit in terms of well-being, and though we suggest that reasoning may be detrimental to well-being *in some cases*, at the same time it may aid other processes of development, such as the development of self-continuity (Pasupathi et al., 2007). These issues surely deserve future theoretical and empirical attention. We humbly close by noting that there is much more literature to connect to in the service of our argument, which is beyond the scope of this chapter. We hope that these ideas serve as stepping stones to enrich the already vibrant conversation about how it is that individuals successfully story the self.

References

Bamberg, M. (2004). Form and functions of "slut bashing" in male identity constructions in 15-year-olds. *Human Development*, *47*, 331–353.

Bauer, J. J., McAdams, D. P., & Sakaeda, A. R. (2005). Crystallization of desire and crystallization of discontent in narratives of life-changing decisions. *Journal of Personality*, *73*(5), 1181–1214.

Baumeister, R. F., Stillwell, A., & Wotman, S. R. (1990). Victim and perpetrator accounts of interpersonal conflict: Autobiographical narratives about anger. *Journal of Personality and Social Psychology*, *59*, 994–1005.

Bird, A., & Reese, E. (2006). Emotional reminiscing and the development of an autobiographical self. *Developmental Psychology*, *42*, 613–626.

Bluck, S., & Gluck, J. (2004). Making things better and learning a lesson: Experiencing wisdom across the lifespan. *Journal of Personality*, *72*, 543–572.

Bonanno, G. A. (2005). Resilience in the face of potential trauma. *Current Directions in Psychological Science*, *14*, 135–138.

Bonanno, G. A., Neria, Y., Mancini, A., Coifman, K. G., Litz, B., & Insel, B. (2007). Is there more to complicated grief than depression and posttraumatic stress disorder? A test of incremental validity. *Journal of Abnormal Psychology*, *116*, 342–351.

Breen, A. V. (2010). How pregnant and parenting young women construct a new self-identity and effect positive change in antisocial behavior. Manuscript in preparation.

Bruner, J. S. (1990). *Acts of meaning*. Cambridge, MA: Harvard University Press.

Carstensen, L. L. (1991). Selectivity theory: Social activity in life-span context. In K. W. Schaie (Ed.), *Annual review of gerontology and geriatrics* (Vol. 11, pp. 195–217). New York: Springer.

Coifman, K. G., Bonanno, G. A., Ray, R. D., & Gross, J. J. (2007). Does repressive coping promote resilience? Affective-autonomic response discrepancy during bereavement. *Journal of Personality and Social Psychology*, *92*, 745–758.

De La Ronde, C., & Swann, W. B. Jr. (1998). Partner verification: Restoring shattered images of our intimates. *Journal of Personality & Social Psychology*, *75*, 374–382.

Fivush, R. (2010). Speaking silence: The social construction of silence in autobiographical and cultural narratives. *Memory*, *18*, 88–98.

Fivush, R., & Baker-Ward, L. (2005). The search for meaning: Developmental perspectives on internal state language in autobiographical memory. *Journal of Cognition and Development, 6*, 455–462.

Fivush, R., Marin, K., Crawford, M., Reynolds, M., & Brewin, C. R. (2007). Children's narratives and well-being. *Cognition & Emotion, 21*, 1414–1434.

Fivush, R., & Sales, J. M. (2006). Coping, attachment, and mother-child narratives of stressful events [Special issue]. *Merrill-Palmer Quarterly, 52*(1), 125–150.

Habermas, T. (2007). How to tell a life: The development of the cultural concept of biography. *Journal of Cognition and Development, 8*, 1–31.

Habermas, T., & Bluck, S. (2000). Getting a life: The emergence of the life story in adolescence. *Psychological Bulletin, 126*, 748–769.

Habermas, T., & de Silveira, C. (2008). The development of global coherence in life narratives across adolescence: Temporal, causal, and thematic aspects. *Developmental Psychology, 3*, 707–721.

Kennedy-Arlin, P. (1990). Wisdom: The art of problem finding. In R. J. Sternberg's (Ed.), *Wisdom: Its nature, origins and development* (pp. 230–243). Cambridge, England: Cambridge University Press.

King, L. A. (2001). The hard road to the good life: The happy, mature person. *Journal of Humanistic Psychology, 41*, 51–72.

King, L. A., Scollon, C. K., Ramsey, C., & Williams, T. (2000). Stories of life transition: Subjective well-being and ego development in parents of children with Down syndrome. *Journal of Research in Personality, 34*, 509–536.

Kitchener, K. S., & Brenner, H. G. (1990). Wisdom and reflective judgment: Knowing in the face of uncertainty. In R. J. Sternberg's (Ed.), *Wisdom: Its nature, origins and development*. Cambridge UK: Cambridge University Press.

Lilgendahl, J. P., & McAdams, D. P. (in press) Constructing growth: How patterns of autobiographical reasoning reveal narrative identity and relate to well-being in midlife adults. *Journal of Personality.*

Loevinger, J. (1976). *Ego development.* San Francisco: Jossey-Bass.

Lyubomirsky, S., Sousa, L., Dickerhoof, R. (2006). The costs and benefits of writing, talking, and thinking about life's triumphs and defeats. *Journal of Personality and Social Psychology, 90*, 692–708.

Mansfield, C. D., McLean, K. C., & Lilgendahl, J. P. (in press). Does narrative processing matter and for whom? Links between narrative processing, wisdom, and well-being in narratives of traumas and transgressions. *Narrative Inquiry.*

Markus, H. R., & Kitayama, S. (1991). Culture and the self: Implications for cognition, emotion, and motivation. *Psychological Review, 98*, 224–253.

McAdams, D. P. (1996). Personality, modernity, and the storied self: A contemporary framework for studying persons. *Psychological Inquiry, 7*(4), 295–321.

McAdams, D. P. (2001). The psychology of life stories. *Review of General Psychology, 5*, 100–122.

McAdams, D. P. (2006). The redemptive self: Generativity and the stories Americans live by. *Research in Human Development, 3*(2–3), 81–100.

McAdams, D. P., Anyidoho, N. A., Brown, C., Huang, Y. T., Kaplan, B., & Machado, M. A. (2004). Traits and stories: Links between dispositional and narrative features of personality. *Journal of Personality, 72*, 761–784.

McLean, K. C. (2008a). The emergence of narrative identity. *Social and Personality Compass, 2*, 1–18.

McLean, K. C. (2008b). Stories of the young and the old: Personal continuity and narrative identity. *Developmental Psychology, 44*, 254–264.

McLean, K. C., Breen, A. V., & Fournier, M. A. (2010). Constructing the self in early, middle, and late adolescent boys: Narrative identity, individuation, and well-being. *Journal of Research on Adolescence*, 166–187.

NEW DIRECTIONS FOR CHILD AND ADOLESCENT DEVELOPMENT • DOI: 10.1002/cd

McLean, K. C., & Fournier, M. A. (2008). The content and processes of autobiographical reasoning in narrative identity. *Journal of Research in Personality*, 42, 527–545.

McLean, K. C., & Lilgendahl, J. P. (2008). Why recall our highs and lows: Relations between memory functions, age, and well-being. *Memory*, 16, 751–762.

McLean, K. C., & Pasupathi, M. (in press). Old, new, borrowed, blue? The emergence and retention of personal meaning in autobiographical storytelling. *Journal of Personality*.

McLean, K. C., Pasupathi, M., & Pals, J. L. (2007). Selves creating stories creating selves: A process model of self-development. *Personality and Social Psychology Review*, 11, 262–278.

McLean, K. C., & Pratt, M. W. (2006). Life's little (and big) lessons: Identity statuses and meaning-making in the turning point narratives of emerging adults. *Developmental Psychology*, 42, 714–722.

McLean, K. C., & Thorne A. (2003). Adolescents' self-defining memories about relationships. *Developmental Psychology*, 30, 635–645.

McLean, K. C., & Thorne, A. (2006). Identity light: Entertainment as a vehicle for self development. In D. P. McAdams, R. Josselson, & A. Lieblich (Eds.), *Identity and story: Creating self in narrative* (pp. 111–127). Washington, DC: APA Press.

Pals, J. L. (2006a). Narrative identity processing of difficult life experiences: Pathways of personality development and positive self-transformation in adulthood. *Journal of Personality*, 74, 1079–1110.

Pals, J. L. (2006b). Constructing the "springboard effect": Causal connections, self-making, and growth within the life story. In D. P. McAdams, R. Josselson, & A. Lieblich (Eds.), *Identity and story: Creating self in narrative* (pp. 175–199). Washington, DC: APA Press.

Pals, J. L., & McAdams, D. P. (2004). The transformed self: A narrative understanding of posttraumatic growth. *Psychological Inquiry*, 15, 65–69.

Pasupathi, M. (2006). Silk from sows ears: Collaborative construction of everyday selves in everyday stories. In D. P. McAdams, R. Josselson, & A. Lieblich (Eds.), *Narrative Study of Lives Self & Identity* (pp. 129–150). Washington, DC: APA Press.

Pasupathi, M., & Hoyt, T. (2009). The development of narrative identity in late adolescence and emergent adulthood: The continued importance of listeners. *Developmental Psychology*, 45, 558–574.

Pasupathi, M., & Mansour, E. (2006). Adult age differences in autobiographical reasoning in narratives. *Developmental Psychology*, 42, 798–808.

Pasupathi, M., Mansour, E., & Brubaker, J. (2007). Developing a life story: Constructing relations between self and experience in autobiographical narratives. *Human Development*, 50, 85–110.

Pasupathi, M., McLean, K. C., & Weeks, T. (2009). To tell or not to tell: Disclosure and the narrative self. *Journal of Personality*, 77, 89–124.

Pennebaker, J. W., & Seagal, J. D. (1999). Forming a story: The health benefits of narrative. *Journal of Clinical Psychology*, 55, 1243–1254.

Polkinghorne, D. E. (2004). Ricoeur, narrative and personal identity. In C. Lightfoot, C. Lalonde, & M. J. Chandler (Eds.), *Changing conceptions of psychological life* (pp. 49–70). Mahwah, NJ: Erlbaum.

Pressman, D. L., & Bonanno, G. A. (2007). With whom do we grieve? Social and cultural determinants of grief processing in the United States and China. *Journal of Social and Personal Relationships*, 24, 729–746.

Ross, M., & Wilson, A. E. (2002). It feels like yesterday: Self-esteem, valence of personal past experiences, and judgments of subjective distance. *Journal of Personality and Social Psychology*, 82, 792–803.

Ross, M., & Wilson, A. E. (2003). Autobiographical memory and conceptions of self: Getting better all the time. *Current Directions in Psychological Science*, 12, 66–69.

Rubenzer, S. J., & Faschingbauer, T. R. (2004). *Personality, character, and leadership in the White House: Psychologists assess the presidents.* Washington, DC: Brassey's.
Thorne, A. (2004). Putting the person into social identity. *Human Development, 253,* 1–5.
Thorne, A., & McLean, K. C. (2003). Telling traumatic events in adolescence: A study of master narrative positioning. In R. Fivush & C. Hayden (Eds.), *Connecting culture and memory the development of an autobiographical self* (pp. 160–186). Mahwah, NJ: Erlbaum.
Thorne, A., McLean, K. C., & Lawrence, A. M. (2004). When remembering is not enough: Reflecting on self-defining memories in late adolescence. *Journal of Personality, 72,* 513–541.
Wang, Q. (2001). Did you have fun? American and Chinese mother–child conversations about shared emotional experiences. *Cognitive Development, 16*(2), 693–715.
Wang, Q., & Brockmeier, J. (2002). Autobiographical remembering as cultural practice: Understanding the interplay between memory, self and culture. *Culture and Psychology, 8,* 45–64.
Westphal, M., & Bonanno, G. A. (2007). Posttraumatic growth and resilience to trauma: Different sides of the same coin or different coins? *Applied Psychology: An International Review, 56,* 417–427.
Weststrate, N. M., & McLean, K. C. (2010). The rise and fall of gay: A cultural-historical approach to gay identity development. *Memory, 18,* 225–240.
Wong, P. T., & Watt. L. M. (1991). What types of reminiscence are associated with successful aging? *Psychology and Aging, 6,* 272–279.

KATE C. MCLEAN *is an assistant professor of psychology at Western Washington University, Bellingham.*

CADE D. MANSFIELD *just completed his MS in experimental psychology at Western Washington University, Bellingham.*

INDEX

study children's moral emotions and moral cognition. They also provide examples illustrating how the principles of integrative moral education can be applied in educational practice.
ISBN 978-04709-03889

CAD128 **Focus on Gender: Parent and Child Contributions to the Socialization of Emotional Competence**
Amy Kennedy Root, Susanne A. Denham, Editors
Gender's influence on human development is all encompassing. In fact, "Virtually all of human functioning has a gendered cast—appearance, mannerisms, communication, temperament, activities at home and outside, aspirations, and values" (Ruble, Martin, & Berenbaum, 2006, p. 858).

In short, gender impacts growth in a multitude of developmental domains, including the development of emotion and emotional competence. Although emotions are, in part, biological, the meanings of emotions and appropriateness of emotional expression are socialized. In the early years of life, socialization primarily takes place via interactions within the family, and characteristics of both parents and children may affect the process of emotion socialization. Gender is one critically important moderator of what and how children learn about emotion because culture determines the appropriateness of emotional displays for males and females.

The goal of this sourcebook is to provide a comprehensive volume addressing what we see as the critical issues in the study of gender, emotion socialization, and the development of emotional competence. Each of the chapters provides evidence for the pervasive role that gender plays in emotional development and provides a framework to better understand the development of emotion in boys and girls.
ISBN 978-04706-47868

CAD127 **Social Anxiety in Childhood: Bridging Developmental and Clinical Perspectives**
Heidi Gazelle, Kenneth H. Rubin, Editors
Social anxiety in childhood is the focus of research in three psychological research traditions: developmental studies emphasizing dispositional constructs such as behavioral inhibition and its biological substrates; developmental investigations emphasizing affective-behavioral characteristics (anxious solitude/withdrawal) and their parent–child and peerrelational precursors and moderators; and clinical investigations of social anxiety disorder (also known as social phobia) emphasizing a variety of etiological factors, diagnosis, and treatment. In this volume, we review and identify gaps in extant evidence that permit (or impede) researchers from the three traditions to translate their core definitional constructs in ways that would facilitate the use of one another's research. Intimately connected to this translation of constructs is a discussion of the conceptualization of core states (anxiety, wariness, solitude) and their manifestations across childhood, as well as corresponding methodologies. Extant research is analyzed from an integrative, overarching framework of developmental psychopathology in which children's adjustment is conceptualized as multiply determined such that children who share certain risks may display diverse adjustment over time (multifinality) and children with diverse risks may develop shared adaptational difficulties over time (equifinality). Finally, key themes for future integrative research are identified and implications for preventative and early intervention in childhood social anxiety are discussed.
ISBN 978-04706-18059

CAD126   **Siblings as Agents of Socialization**
          Laurie Kramer, Katherine J. Conger, Editors
          Siblings have considerable influence on children's development, yet most
          human development research has neglected the investigation of sibling
          socialization in favor of a focus on parental socialization. This volume uses a
          family systems framework to examine the ways in which siblings contribute
          uniquely to one another's social and emotional development. The
          groundbreaking lines of research in this volume address mechanisms by
          which children are influenced by their sisters and brothers, ways in which
          these processes of sibling socialization are similar to and different from those
          with parents, and conditions under which sibling socialization has positive
          versus negative impact on individual development. Throughout this volume,
          attention is devoted to contextual factors that moderate sibling influences,
          such as family structure, life course events, ethnicity and culture, gender, and
          demographic indicators.
          ISBN 978-04706-14594

CAD125   **Evidentiality: A Window Into Language and Cognitive Development**
          Stanka A. Fitneva, Tomoko Matsui, Editors
          Much recent research investigates children's understanding of the sources of
          human knowledge and the relation of this understanding to socio-cognitive
          development. This volume of *New Directions for Child and Adolescent Devel-
          opment* highlights new research in this area that focuses on evidentials:
          word affixes and sentence particles that indicate the speaker's source of
          knowledge—for example, perception, inference, or hearsay. Evidentials are
          a feature of about a quarter of the languages in the world and have a vari-
          ety of interesting characteristics. For example, in contrast to lexical alter-
          natives familiar from English, such as "I saw," they are extremely frequent.
          The volume brings together scholars pioneering research on evidentiality
          in Bulgarian, Japanese, Tibetan, and Turkish. Their contributions to this
          volume provide a glimpse at the diversity of evidential systems around
          the globe while examining a number of provocative questions: How do
          evidentials mediate children's acquisition of knowledge from others' testi-
          mony? What is the relation between grammaticalized and lexical expres-
          sions of source of knowledge? Does the acquisition of an evidential system
          boost source monitoring and inferential skills? The volume is a compelling
          illustration of the relevance of evidentiality to broadening our understand-
          ing of development in many domains, including theory of mind, memory,
          and knowledge acquisition.
          ISBN 978-04705-69658

CAD124   **Coping and the Development of Regulation**
          Ellen A. Skinner, Melanie J. Zimmer-Gembeck, Editors
          A developmental conceptualization that emphasizes coping as regulation
          under stress opens the way to explore synergies between coping and regu-
          latory processes, including self-regulation; behavioral, emotion, attention,
          and action regulation; ego control; self-control; compliance; and volition. This
          volume, with chapters written by experts on the development of regulation
          and coping during childhood and adolescence, is the first to explore these
          synergies. The volume is geared toward researchers working in the broad
          areas of regulation, coping, stress, adversity, and resilience. For regulation
          researchers, it offers opportunities to focus on age-graded changes in how
          these processes function under stress and to consider multiple targets of
          regulation simultaneously—emotion, attention, behavior—that typically are

examined in isolation. For researchers interested in coping, this volume offers invigorating theoretical and operational ideas. For researchers studying stress, adversity, and resilience, the volume highlights coping as one pathway through which exposure to adversity shapes children's long-term development. The authors also address cross-cutting developmental themes, such as the role of stress, coping, and social relationships in the successive integration of regulatory subsystems, the emergence of autonomous regulation, and the progressive construction of the kinds of regulatory resources and routines that allow flexible constructive coping under successively higher levels of stress and adversity. All chapters emphasize the importance of integrative multilevel perspectives in bringing together work on the neurobiology of stress, temperament, attachment, regulation, personal resources, relationships, stress exposure, and social contexts in studying processes of coping, adversity, and resilience.
ISBN 978-04705-31372

CAD 123 *Social Interaction and the Development of Executive Function*
Charlie Lewis, Jeremy I. M. Carpendale, Editors
Executive function consists of higher cognitive skills that are involved in the control of thought, action, and emotion. It has been linked to neural systems involving the prefrontal cortex, but a full definition of the term has remained elusive partly because it includes such a complex set of cognitive processes. Relatively little is known about the processes that promote development of executive function, and how it is linked to children's social behavior. The key factor examined by the chapters in this issue is the role of social interaction, and the chapters take an increasingly broad perspective. Two end pieces introduce the topic as a whole (Chapter 1) and present an integrative commentary on the articles (Chapter 6) in an attempt to stress the social origins of executive function, in contrast to many contemporary cognitive approaches. The empirical contributions in between examine the roles of parental scaffolding of young preschoolers (Chapter 2), the links between maternal education and conversational support (Chapter 3), how such family background factors and social skills extend into adolescence (Chapter 4), and wider cultural influences (Chapter 5) on development of executive skills. This volume is aimed at a broad range of developmental researchers and practitioners interested in the influences of family background and interactions as well as educational and cultural processes on development of the child's self-control and social understanding. Such relationships have wide implications for many aspects of the lives of children and adolescents.
ISBN 978-04704-89017

CAD 122 *Core Competencies to Prevent Problem Behaviors and Promote Positive Youth Development*
Nancy G. Guerra, Catherine P. Bradshaw, Editors
Adolescence generally is considered a time of experimentation and increased involvement in risk or problem behaviors, including early school leaving, violence, substance use, and high-risk sexual behavior. In this volume, the authors show how individual competencies linked to well-being can reduce youth involvement in these risk behaviors. Five core competencies are emphasized: a positive sense of self, self-control, decision-making skills, a moral system of belief, and prosocial connectedness. A central premise of this volume is that high levels of the core competencies provide a marker for positive youth development, whereas low levels increase the likelihood of adolescent risk behavior. The authors summarize the empirical literature linking these competencies to each risk behavior, providing examples from

developmental and prevention research. They highlight programs and policies in the United States and internationally that have changed one or more dimensions of the core competencies through efforts designed to build individual skills, strengthen relationships, and enhance opportunities and supports across multiple developmental contexts.

ISBN 978-04704-42166

CAD 121 **Beyond the Family: Contexts of Immigrant Children's Development**
Hirokazu Yoshikawa, Niobe Way, Editors

Immigration in the United States has become a central focus of policy and public concern in the first decade of the 21st century. This volume aims to broaden developmental research on children and youth in immigrant families. Much of the research on immigrant children and youth concentrates on family characteristics such as parenting, demographic, or human capital features. In this volume, we consider the developmental consequences for immigrant youth of broader contexts such as social networks, peer discrimination in school and out-of-school settings, legal contexts, and access to institutional resources. Chapters answer questions such as: How do experiences of discrimination affect the lives of immigrant youth? How do social networks of immigrant families influence children's learning? How do immigrant parents' citizenship status influence family life and their children's development? In examining factors as disparate as discrimination based on physical appearance, informal adult helpers, and access to drivers' licenses, these chapters serve to enrich our notions of how culture and context shape human development, as well as inform practice and public policy affecting immigrant families.

ISBN 978-04704-17300

CAD 120 **The Intersections of Personal and Social Identities**
Margarita Azmitia, Moin Syed, Kimberley Radmacher, Editors

This volume brings together an interdisciplinary set of social scientists who are pioneering ways to research and theorize the connections between personal and social identity development in children, adolescents, and emerging adults. The authors of the seven chapters address the volume's three goals: (1) illustrating how theory and research in identity develop-ment are enriched by an interdisciplinary approach, (2) providing a rich developmental picture of personal and social identity development, and (3) examining the connections among multiple identities. Several chapters provide practical suggestions for individuals, agencies, and schools and universities that work with children, adolescents, and emerging adults in diverse communities across the United States.

ISBN 978-04703-72838

NEW DIRECTIONS FOR CHILD AND ADOLESCENT DEVELOPMENT

ORDER FORM SUBSCRIPTION AND SINGLE ISSUES

DISCOUNTED BACK ISSUES:

Use this form to receive 20% off all back issues of *New Directions for Child and Adolescent Development*. All single issues priced at **$23.20** (normally $29.00)

TITLE	ISSUE NO.	ISBN

Call 888-378-2537 or see mailing instructions below. When calling, mention the promotional code JBNND to receive your discount. For a complete list of issues, please visit www.josseybass.com/go/ndcad

SUBSCRIPTIONS: (1 YEAR, 4 ISSUES)

☐ New Order   ☐ Renewal

U.S.	☐ Individual: $89	☐ Institutional: $315
CANADA/MEXICO	☐ Individual: $89	☐ Institutional: $355
ALL OTHERS	☐ Individual: $113	☐ Institutional: $389

Call 888-378-2537 or see mailing and pricing instructions below.
Online subscriptions are available at www.onlinelibrary.wiley.com

ORDER TOTALS:

Issue / Subscription Amount: $ _____

Shipping Amount: $ _____
(for single issues only – subscription prices include shipping)

Total Amount: $ _____

SHIPPING CHARGES:

First Item	$5.00
Each Add'l Item	$3.00

(No sales tax for U.S. subscriptions. Canadian residents, add GST for subscription orders. Individual rate subscriptions must be paid by personal check or credit card. Individual rate subscriptions may not be resold as library copies.)

BILLING & SHIPPING INFORMATION:

☐ **PAYMENT ENCLOSED:** *(U.S. check or money order only. All payments must be in U.S. dollars.)*

☐ **CREDIT CARD:**   ☐ VISA   ☐ MC   ☐ AMEX

Card number _____ Exp. Date _____

Card Holder Name _____ Card Issue # _____

Signature _____ Day Phone _____

☐ **BILL ME:** *(U.S. institutional orders only. Purchase order required.)*

Purchase order # _____
Federal Tax ID 13559302 • GST 89102-8052

Name _____

Address _____

Phone _____ E-mail _____

Copy or detach page and send to: **John Wiley & Sons, PTSC, 5th Floor**
989 Market Street, San Francisco, CA 94103-1741

Order Form can also be faxed to: **888-481-2665**

PROMO JBNND